MY FIRST HISTORY

LEVEL K

MY FIRST HISTORY

Exciting Stories of God's People

BY R.A. SHEATS & JOSHUA SCHWISOW

Copyright © 2024 by Generations

All rights reserved.
Printed in the United States of America
First Printing, 2024.

ISBN: 978-1-954745-63-6

Unless otherwise noted, Scripture is taken from the New King James Version®. Copyright © 1982 by Thomas Nelson. Used by permission. All rights reserved.

Scripture marked "ESV" is taken from the The ESV Bible (The Holy Bible, English Standard Version), Copyright © 2001 by Crossway, a publishing ministry of Good News Publishers. Used by permission. All rights reserved.

Cover Design: Justin Turley
Cover Illustration: Cedric Hohnstadt
Typesetting: Kyle Shepherd

Published by:
Generations
19039 Plaza Drive Ste 210
Parker, Colorado 80134
www.generations.org

For more information on this and
other titles from Generations,
visit www.generations.org or call 888-389-9080.

CONTENTS

Introduction ix

CHAPTER 1
Miriam and the Bad King of Egypt 1

CHAPTER 2
Josiah: A Little Boy Becomes a King 7

CHAPTER 3
Rhoda Hears a Knock 13

CHAPTER 4
Nicholas of Myra and a Surprise Present 17

CHAPTER 5
A Very Bad Little Boy: Augustine and the Pear Tree 23

CHAPTER 6
Stephen of Perm: A Home in the Cold Mountains 29

CHAPTER 7
Hans Sachs the Shoemaker 35

CHAPTER 8
Marie Viret and a Big, Iron Bell 41

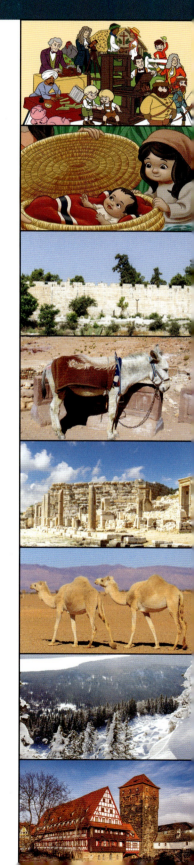

CHAPTER 9
Gustavus Adolphus: King of the Swedes 49

CHAPTER 10
Sir Isaac Newton: Science for God's Glory 57

CHAPTER 11
George Frederic Handel: Making Music and Helping Children 65

CHAPTER 12
Rajanaiken Finds a Very Special Book 71

CHAPTER 13
Khanee and the New Shoes 77

CHAPTER 14
Bartimaeus Puaaiki, the Blind Boy of Hawaii 83

CHAPTER 15
Samuel Morse: Artist and Inventor 89

CHAPTER 16
Betty Moves to a New Home 99

CHAPTER 17
Elias Boudinot and His Printing Press 107

CONTENTS

CHAPTER 18
Cyrus McCormick and His Reaper 113

CHAPTER 19
Louis Pasteur: A Scientist Helps a Sick Little Boy 121

CHAPTER 20
Charles Spurgeon and His Grandfather 127

CHAPTER 21
Joseph Neesima: A Soldier or a Teacher? 133

CHAPTER 22
Kahi Gets Married 137

CHAPTER 23
George Washington Carver Finds a Special Gift from God 145

CHAPTER 24
Fa-Ying of Siam: A Princess and a Very Special Person 151

CHAPTER 25
Mary Slessor: The Red-Haired Lady and the Twin Babies 157

CHAPTER 26
Chi Wang: Mother in the Faith to the Sediq Christians 165

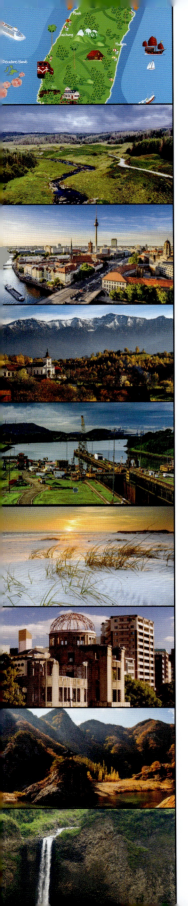

CHAPTER 27
Alexander Fleming Rescues the Sheep 171

CHAPTER 28
Dietrich Bonhoeffer: Roller Skates and a Very Sad War 179

CHAPTER 29
Sabina Wurmbrand Suffers for Jesus 185

CHAPTER 30
A Fight with Mosquitoes: William Gorgas in Panama 195

CHAPTER 31
Jim Sledge and a Special Pet 203

CHAPTER 32
Myeko Nakamura's House Falls Down 211

CHAPTER 33
Russell Blaisdell Helps the Children 217

CHAPTER 34
Dayuma: Delivered from a Life of Fear 225

INTRODUCTION

Studying the works of God in the past is always a fascinating and rewarding task. By studying history, we learn of God's mighty deeds upon the earth and how He uses faithful men and women in His kingdom work. Amazing stories of God's works inspire us to worship, honor, and praise our glorious King Jesus and to press forward in the work He has set before us.

My First History records some of the most remarkable and memorable stories of God's work in history. A special feature of this introductory history volume is the focus it gives to the role of children in God's kingdom purposes. Many of the stories in *My First History* showcase the childhood of real kids that God used and prepared for His purposes. It is our hope that these stories will encourage children to remember their Creator in the days of their youth (Ecclesiastes 12:1) and to serve the Lord Jesus from an early age.

My First History is designed to introduce children ages 4-6 to the joy and wonder of learning about history. To this end, it covers stories from many different centuries in many different places. There are names of people who are well-known in history, and names that are far less familiar to most. By including such a variety, we want children to understand that God has a purpose for every single one of us.

As Psalm 139 says:

Your eyes saw my unformed substance;
in your book were written, every one of them,
the days that were formed for me,
when as yet there was none of them. (Psalm 139:16 ESV)

God uses men and women of all walks of life to build His church and extend His kingdom on earth. Children will learn how children, queens, scientists, musicians, pastors, mothers, explorers, missionaries, fathers, soldiers, kings, and even samurai warriors are used by God to glorify Himself. Old men and little children, housewives and noblemen are all a part of God's marvelous work of redemptive history.

THE SCOPE OF THIS VOLUME

My First History contains the following biographical accounts. Included on the table below are details about the location and approximate time period covered in each chapter.

Chapter	Name	Location	Time Period
1	Miriam and Moses	Egypt	1500s BC
2	King Josiah	Israel and Judah	600s BC
3	Rhoda and Peter	Israel	1st century
4	Nicholas of Myra	Turkey	3rd century
5	Augustine of Hippo	North Africa	4th century
6	Stephen of Perm	Russia	14th century
7	Hans Sachs	Germany	16th century
8	Marie Viret	Switzerland	16th century
9	Gustavus Adolphus	Sweden	17th century
10	Sir Isaac Newton	England	17th and 18th centuries
11	George Frederic Handel	England	18th century
12	Rajanaiken	India	18th century
13	Khanee	Persia	19th century
14	Puaaiki Bartimaeus	Hawaii	18th century
15	Samuel Morse	USA	19th century
16	Betty Schneider	USA	19th century
17	Elias Boudinot	Cherokee Tribe in USA	19th century
18	Cyrus McCormick	USA	19th century
19	Louis Pasteur	France	19th century
20	Charles Spurgeon	England	19th century

21	Joseph Hardy Neesima	Japan	19th century
22	Kahi and Ropu	Vanuatu	19th century
23	George Washington Carver	USA	19th century
24	Princess Fa-Ying	Thailand	19th century
25	Mary Slessor	Nigeria	19th century
26	Chi Wang	Taiwan	19th century
27	Alexander Fleming	Scotland	20th century
28	Dietrich Bonhoeffer	Germany	20th century
29	Sabina Wurmbrand	Romania	20th century
30	William Gorgas	Panama	20th century
31	Jim Sledge	Philippines	20th century
32	Myeko Nakamura	Japan	20th century
33	Russell Blaisdell	Korea	20th century
34	Dayuma	Ecuador	20th century

THE IMPORTANCE OF PARENTS IN EDUCATION

The study of history is paramount in a child's education. However, studying history is not an end in itself. Though children will learn much from this book, much more is required to truly instill in them an understanding of history and of their place in God's glorious work of redemptive history.

This book is merely a tool to be used. The primary means by which a young child will grow in the knowledge of himself, the world around him, and God is through meaningful conversations with his father and mother. This book has been produced with the intention of providing a suitable platform and opportunity to stimulate and foster such conversations. Parents are encouraged to discuss each chapter with their child using the included discussion questions, drawing out the principles contained in it and assisting their child in putting into practice the lessons they learn.

Studying the history of a fallen world will necessarily involve confronting challenging and sorrowful events such as death, war, violence, persecution, and various other evils. In preparing this volume for young students, we have sought to present these stories at an age-appropriate level by not using graphic descriptions, and by not providing a level of detail that would be too frightening for a 5-7 year old child. However, we recognize that the needs of each child are different depending on their particular maturity level, as well as what they themselves may have already experienced in their lives. Parents/teachers are encouraged to review the content of each story ahead of time should they be concerned that any subject matter may be difficult for the student. If necessary, parents/teachers may adjust what details they read aloud accordingly. Chapters that contain somewhat more difficult subject matter include the following: Fa-Ying (death of a young child), Sabina Wurmbrand (persecution and imprisonment), Myeko Nakamura (a child experiencing wartime bombing), Russell Blaisdell (orphans experiencing wartime conditions), and Dayuma (growing up amidst tribal violence).

SOURCES FOR THE STORIES CONTAINED IN THIS BOOK

Below is a list of sources that were used in the retelling of the stories contained in *My First History*.

Material for the first three chapters cover biblical history and are taken from the inspired and infallible Scriptures of the Old and New Testaments.

Many variations of Nicholas of Myra's life exist. The version given in the chapter in this book is based on the account in Joe Wheeler, *Saint Nicholas* (Thomas Nelson, 2010).

The chapter on Augustine's life has been drawn from Augustine's autobiography contained in his *Confessions,* particularly Books 1, 2, and 8.

The history of Stephen of Perm has been taken from various histories of Russia, including *Some Links in the Chain of Russian Church History* by W. H. Frere (London: Faith Press, 1918) and *A Short History of the Church of Russia* by Rev. Reginald F. Bigg-Wither (New York: The MacMillan Company, 1920).

Information for the chapter on Hans Sachs was drawn from Hans Sachs, *Merry Tales and Three Shrovetide Plays* (trans. William Leighton, London: David Nutt, 1910), and Annis S. Shaver et al., *Staging Luther: Four Plays by Hans Sachs* (Minneapolis: Fortress Press, 2023).

Marie Viret's life was taken from information gathered from the letters of her father Pierre Viret as well as material in Jean Barnaud, *Pierre Viret, sa vie et son oeuvre: 1511-1571* (Saint-Amans: G. Carayol, 1911).

The account of Gustavus Adolphus' life has been taken from Harriet Earhart Monroe's *History of the Life of Gustavus Adolphus II: The Hero-General of the Reformation* (Philadelphia: The Lutheran Publication Society, 1910).

The account of Isaac Newton's life and work has been taken from Mitch Stokes, *Isaac Newton: Christian Encounters Series* (Nashville: Thomas Nelson, 2010).

The story of Handel's life was drawn from Paul Henry Lang, *George Frideric Handel* (New York: W. W. Norton & Company, 1966).

Rajanaiken's story is taken from a letter he wrote in 1732 and published in J. Ferd. Fenger, *History of the Tranquebar Mission Worked out from the Original Papers* (Madras: M. E. Press, 1906).

Khanee's history is drawn from D. T. Fiske, *Faith Working by Love: As Exemplified in the Life of Fidelia Fiske* (Boston: Congregational Sabbath School and Publishing Society, 1868), Thomas Laurie, *Woman and Her Saviour in Persia* (Boston: Gould and Lincoln, 1863), and William Guest, *Fidelia Fiske: The Story of a Consecrated Life* (London: Morgan & Chase, 1870).

The history of Puaaiki Bartimaeus is taken from Hiram Bingham, *A Residence of Twenty-One Years in the Sandwich Islands* (Charles E. Tuttle Company, 1981) and J. S. Green, *Notices of the Life, Character, and Labors of the Late Bartimeus L. Puaaiki* (Lahainaluna: Press of the Mission Seminary, 1844).

The account of Samuel Morse's life and work has been taken from *Samuel F.B. Morse: His Letters and Journals* (1914).

The history of Elizabeth "Betty" Schneider and her family is taken from Ezra E. Eby, *A Biographical History of Waterloo Township and other Townships of the County*, 2 volumes (Ontario: 1895-1896). Some liberty has been taken in adding conversational content to the story.

Elias Boudinot's story has been drawn from Althea Bass, *Cherokee Messenger* (University of Oklahoma Press, 1996).

The account of Cyrus McCormick's life and his inventions has been taken from Herbert N. Casson's *Cyrus McCormick: His Life and Work* (Chicago: A.C. McClurg & Co., 1909).

Material for Louis Pasteur's chapter was taken from Patrice Debré, *Louis Pasteur* (trans. Elborg Forster, Baltimore: John Hopkins University Press, 1994) and Albert Keim, *Louis Pasteur: 1822-1895* (New York: Frederick A. Stokes Company, 1914).

The story of Charles Spurgeon at his grandfather's house is taken from Spurgeon's writings published in *Memories of Stambourne* (Pasadena, Texas: Pilgrim Publications, 1975). The preaching scene is drawn from a sermon Spurgeon preached entitled "All of Grace."

Joseph Hardy Neesima's chapter was drawn from material in Jesse Page, *Japan: Its People and Missions* (Fleming H. Revell Company, n.d.).

Kahi's story and details of life on Aniwa are taken from Margaret Paton's *Letters from the South Seas* (Edinburgh: Banner of Truth Trust, 2003) and John G. Paton's *Autobiography* (Edinburgh: Banner of Truth Trust, 1965).

The details of the chapter on George Washington Carver have been taken from Carver's letters, papers, and speeches recorded in William J. Federer, *George Washington Carver: His Life and Faith in His Own Words* (Amerisearch, Inc., 2002). In Dr. Carver's letters, he does not include the name of the five-year-old patient mentioned in this book. A fictitious name (Teddy) has therefore been supplied.

Princess Fa-Ying's life was drawn from Anna Leonowens, *The English Governess at the Siamese Court* (Oxford University Press, 1988).

The history of Mary Slessor was taken from W. P. Livingstone, *Mary Slessor* (New Jersey: Barbour and Company, Inc., 1986).

The story of Chi Wang and her missionary work among the Sediq people is taken from Margaret L. Copland's booklet *Chi-Oang: Mother of the Taiwan Tribes Church* (Taipei, Taiwan: General Assembly of the Presbyterian Church of Formosa, 1962).

Alexander Fleming's story was drawn from Kevin Brown, *Penicillin Man: Alexander Fleming and the Antibiotic Revolution* (Gloucestershire: History Press, 2013) and L. J. Ludovici, *Fleming: Discoverer of Penicillin* (London: Andrew Dakers Limited, 1952).

Details of Dietrich Bonhoeffer's childhood have been drawn from Eberhard Bethge's biography, *Dietrich Bonhoeffer: A Biography* (Minneapolis: Fortress Press, 2000).

The story of William Gorgas was drawn from Marie D. Gorgas and Burton J. Hendrick, *William Crawford Gorgas: His Life and Work* (New York: Cosimo Classics, 2022).

Introduction xv

The story of Sabina Wurmbrand is based upon the accounts provided in Richard Wurmbrand, *Tortured for Christ: 50th Anniversary* Edition (Colorado Springs: David C. Cook, 2017) and Sabina Wurmbrand, *The Pastor's Wife* (Living Sacrifice Book Co., 2013).

Material for the Jim Sledge chapter was taken from R. A. Sheats, *Just Jim: A Little Boy, a Time of Trouble, and a Faithful God* (Monticello: Psalm 78 Ministries, 2021) as well as personal interviews with Dr. Jim Sledge.

The details of Myeko Nakamura and her family's experiences were taken from John Hersey, *Hiroshima* (New York: Alfred A. Knopf, 1946).

The story of Chaplain Russell L. Blaisdell was drawn from Blaisdell's reports of his time in Korea, news stories that appeared in the 1950s in *Pacific Stars and Stripes*, and material available from Koreanchildren.org.

The story of Dayuma of the Waorani is taken from Ethel Emily Wallis' *Dayuma: Life Under Waorani Spears* (Seattle: YWAM Publishing, 1996).

SCHEDULE

Parents/teachers may complete this book with their student at their own pace. However, for a 36-week school year, parents/teachers may consider reading one chapter aloud each week and discussing the questions with their student. At this pace, the book can be completed in 34 weeks.

CONCLUSION

It is our prayer that these tales of the boys and girls, men and women of the past will inspire and encourage a new generation to stand strong in the good fight as they continually look to Jesus, the Author and Finisher of their faith!

R.A. Sheats and Joshua Schwisow
The Generations Curriculum Team
May 2024

MIRIAM AND THE BAD KING OF EGYPT

Miriam was a little girl. She lived with her mommy and daddy in a land called Egypt. It was hot in Egypt. The sun shone bright and strong. When Miriam went outside, the sand was hot on her feet.

Miriam and her family lived in Egypt, but they were not Egyptians. They were Israelites. They were part of the people of Israel. The Israelites lived in Egypt, but they wanted to leave Egypt. The Israelites wanted to live in their own land.

Why do you think they wanted to leave Egypt? They were sad there. The king of Egypt did not like the Israelites. He did bad things to them. The Israelites were sad, and they prayed to God. They said, "God, please rescue us from the king of Egypt. Please let us leave Egypt and live in our own land where we will be free."

Miriam listened as her mommy and daddy prayed. She wondered, "When will God answer our prayers? When will He rescue us?"

Miriam had a brother named Aaron. One day, Miriam's mother had another baby boy. Miriam was glad to have another brother. She liked to help take care of the baby. He was a beautiful little boy. But Miriam's mother knew the king of Egypt would be angry if he found the baby. "We have to hide your baby brother," she told Miriam. "We don't want the king to find out about our little baby boy."

Miriam's mother put the baby inside a special basket. She hid the basket beside the river. Miriam stayed by the river and kept watch to be sure her baby brother was safe. She wondered, "What will happen to him? Will he die?"

Suddenly, Miriam saw a woman coming down to the river. The woman was an Egyptian. The bad king of Egypt was her father. Do you think Miriam was afraid of her?

The Egyptian woman was a princess. She looked around at the river. Then she saw the basket in the reeds. Miriam watched while the princess opened the basket and looked inside. What did she see?

"A baby!" the princess said with surprise. The baby felt surprised as well. The baby began to cry. The Egyptian princess smiled. "Poor little baby!" she said. "He's hungry. I must find someone to take care of him."

Miriam heard what the princess said, so she walked up to her. "Do you want me to go find someone to feed the baby?" she asked. "My mommy can give the baby some milk to drink."

"Yes, go bring your mother," the princess said. Miriam ran back to her house and called her mother. The princess gave the baby to Miriam's mother. The princess didn't know the baby belonged to her. "Take this baby and feed him," the princess said. "I want to keep him safe, and he will be my own son."

The mother took good care of her baby boy. When he grew older, the princess took the little boy to live with her. They lived in her big Egyptian house. She called the baby Moses.

LEARNING TO BE PATIENT

Miriam was glad her brother was safe, but she didn't want him to live in Egypt. She didn't want to live in Egypt with the bad king, either!

The Egyptian princess found Moses beside the Nile River.

Every day, Miriam and the people of Israel prayed. They asked God to rescue them from the bad king of Egypt. Did God hear their prayer?

Miriam waited a long time. She wondered, "Will God answer our prayer today? Will He save us today?" No, God didn't save them that day. And on the next day, Miriam wondered, "Will God rescue us today?" But God didn't rescue them that day either.

It took a long, long time of waiting before God rescued them. Miriam knew she had to be patient, but it was hard to be patient. At last, God said, "My people, Israel, are in Egypt. I have heard them cry because the Egyptians hurt them. I have seen their pain. I will rescue them from the king of Egypt."

Miriam was so happy to leave Egypt. She was so happy that she sang a song to praise God. She held a tambourine in her hand and sang and danced. She sang: "Sing to the Lord, for He has done great things!" The rest of the Israelites joined Miriam. They sang, "The Lord is my strength and song. The Lord will reign forever and ever!"

WHAT HAPPENED LATER?

God rescued the Israelites from Egypt. He stopped the king of Egypt from hurting them. Then God gave the Israelites a new land. It was the land of Israel.

Miriam was so thankful God answered their prayers. She was thankful He set her people free. She was thankful He rescued them from the bad king. She had had to be patient, but God had been faithful. God had kept His promise and given them a new home in Israel.

I waited patiently for the Lord;
And He inclined to me,
And heard my cry.
(Psalm 40:1)

DISCUSSION QUESTIONS

1. What did Miriam's mommy do when baby Moses was born?
2. Was the king of Egypt a good king or a bad king?
3. Why did Miriam have to be patient?
4. What does our Bible verse teach us?

Miriam lived in the land of Egypt. Egypt was a hot place to live.

Jerusalem, Israel

JOSIAH: A LITTLE BOY BECOMES A KING

After Miriam and the people of Israel left the land of Egypt, they moved to a land God gave them. This was the land of Israel. Do you see it on the map? Israel is close to Egypt.

A king ruled over the people in the land of Israel. One day, the king died, and it was time for a new king to rule over the people. Who do you think the new king was? He was a little boy named Josiah. Josiah was only eight years old when he became king.

Do you think Josiah was excited to be a king? Do you think he knew how to be a king? He may have needed some help from the surrounding adults. They could help him learn how to be a good king.

If you were a king or a queen, would you know what to do? Would you know what is right and what is wrong? Could you teach all the people to do good things and not bad things? That would be difficult! Josiah had a hard job. It is not easy to be a king.

FINDING A LOST BOOK

One day, King Josiah asked some men to clean up the temple. The temple was the place where people came to worship God. The men started cleaning each room in the temple. When they went into one room, they found an old book. This was a book Moses wrote. It had all the laws God gave His people. These laws told the people how they should live.

A man brought this book to the king. "King Josiah, we have found the Book of God's Law!" the man said.

Josiah was excited to see the book. He said, "We must read this book. It will tell us how God wants us to live."

The man read the book to Josiah. As he read, Josiah said, "God's Law is good, but we have not done what God told us to do. We have not obeyed God. We have done bad things." Josiah started to cry. He was sorry the people of Israel had done bad things. He wanted everyone to do good things just like God's perfect Law told them to.

What do you think King Josiah did? He called all the rulers of the people together. Then he called all the fathers and mothers and boys and girls. He told them to come to a big meeting. When all the people had arrived, King Josiah stood up and started to read. He read the Book of God's Law to the people. All the people listened as the king read the words of the book.

What would you do if you were a king or a queen?

When Josiah was king, books were written on long pieces of paper called scrolls.

When King Josiah finished reading all the book, he spoke to the people. He said, "We must obey what God wrote in this book. We must obey all the laws and commandments that God gave us. In His book, God told us how to live. We must obey Him."

The people said, "The king is right. We must obey God! We must do what His Law tells us to do."

DOING WHAT IS RIGHT

Is it good for you to fight with your brother or sister? Is it good for you to take something that does not belong to you? King Josiah told the people that these things were wrong. "God's Law tells us not to take things that are not ours," he told the people. "We must obey God's Law because it is a perfect Law."

Josiah tore his clothes in grief when he heard God's Law.

Josiah loved God with his whole heart and wanted to live exactly like God told him to. He wanted to be a good king and lead his people well. But at times, it was hard to know what to do. At times, he did not know what was right and what was wrong. Is there a way he could find out? Do you know?

If Josiah did not know what to do, he could look in God's Book. God's Book teaches what is right and what is wrong. Do you know what we call God's Book today? We call it the Bible.

Josiah loved to read God's Book and to think about it. Another word for thinking about something is *meditating*. If we *meditate* on God's Law, that means we think about it all the time. We think about how to love God and obey Him and how to do what is right.

Oh, how I love Your law! It is my meditation all the day. (Psalm 119:97)

DISCUSSION QUESTIONS

1. How old was Josiah when he became king?
2. What book did the men find when they were cleaning the temple?
3. How did Josiah know what was right and what was wrong?
4. What does our Bible verse say we should do if we love God's Law?

Some people in Jerusalem traveled on donkeys. Would you like to ride a donkey?

RHODA HEARS A KNOCK

Jerusalem was a big city. Many people lived there. Many animals lived there as well. There were no cars or trucks or airplanes in Jerusalem in the past. But there were horses and donkeys. If you wanted to visit a friend, you would ride a donkey—or you would walk. But you could not ride in a car or on a bicycle. Jerusalem did not have cars or bicycles yet!

A long time ago, a bad king ruled over Jerusalem. His name was Herod. Herod was not a good man. He did many bad things. People did not like Herod because of the bad things he did.

Some of the people who lived in Jerusalem were God's people. They loved Jesus very much. Peter was one of these people. He loved Jesus and wanted to obey Him.

When Jesus was on earth, Peter followed Him and listened to Him talk. Peter learned many things as he listened. He learned that Jesus is God. He learned that God made all things, and God loves everything He made. He learned that Jesus loved His people so much He came to earth to save them! Peter's heart overflowed with love for his Savior Jesus.

With Jesus in heaven once more, Peter lived in Jerusalem. Peter told as many people as possible about God. These people gathered to pray, to sing, and to learn more about Jesus. One of them was a girl named Rhoda. Rhoda and Peter were friends.

But one day, a bad thing happened. King Herod sent his soldiers to arrest Peter. The soldiers put Peter in prison.

When Rhoda found out about

Peter, she was afraid. She did not want bad King Herod to hurt Peter or to lock him up in prison.

Many Christians lived in Jerusalem. The Christians heard that Peter was in prison. They gathered in a house. They began to pray and ask God for help. They asked God to rescue Peter from prison.

While they prayed, God did something. Can you guess what He did? He rescued Peter from the prison and set him free. With God's help, Peter escaped from King Herod! Peter was out of prison, but none of his friends, the Christians, knew this. They did not know God had set Peter free. The Christians remained in the house praying. Peter thought, "I need to tell my friends that I am free!"

Peter went to the house and tried to go in. But the Christians had locked the gate. They were afraid King Herod might send more soldiers to arrest them. Peter knocked on the door. *Knock, knock, knock.* "Let me in!" he said.

Rhoda heard someone knocking at the gate, so she went to see who was knocking. "Who is there?" she asked. Do you think Rhoda thought it was a soldier trying to arrest her? But Rhoda listened, and she did not hear a soldier's voice. She heard the voice of a friend!

"It is me. It is Peter."

"Peter?" thought Rhoda. She recognized his voice and knew that it *was* Peter! He was free! Rhoda was so happy. She ran back into the house to tell all the people the good news. Rhoda was so excited that she forgot to open the gate and let Peter in.

Rhoda raced into the room where all the Christians were praying. "Peter is at the door!" she cried out.

The people looked at Rhoda in surprise. "Peter cannot be at the door," they said. "He is locked up in prison."

"But I heard him!" Rhoda said.

The people shook their heads. "No, it cannot be Peter," they repeated.

Then they heard something. Peter was still standing outside the house, knocking. *Knock, knock, knock!*

"It *is* Peter!" Rhoda insisted. "He is at the door right now! Come and see!"

Finally, one of Peter's friends opened the gate to look. "It is Peter!" they cried, overjoyed. "God has answered our prayers! Peter is free!"

That was a big surprise. God heard His people pray, and He saved Peter from prison. Rhoda and all the Christians thanked God for answering their prayer.

The Lord is near to all who call upon Him, to all who call upon Him in truth. (Psalm 145:18)

DISCUSSION QUESTIONS

1. How did people in Peter's city travel? Did they ride in a car?
2. What did King Herod do to Peter?
3. What did Rhoda and the other Christians do?
4. Did the people believe Rhoda when she said Peter was at the door?
5. What does our Bible verse teach us?

The ancient city of Patara

NICHOLAS OF MYRA AND A SURPRISE PRESENT

4

Do you remember Paul the Apostle? He lived a long, long time ago. He was a friend of Peter, the man we learned about in the last chapter. Paul traveled all over the Greek and Roman world. He wanted to tell everyone about Jesus. One of the places he traveled to was a region called Lycia.

The people in Lycia learned about God from Paul. Paul taught them that Jesus Christ had come to save them from their sins. The Lycians learned that if they trusted in the Lord Jesus, they would be saved. They began to love God and obey Him. One day, a little boy was born in Lycia. The little boy's mommy and daddy named him Nicholas. Nicholas was born about 270 years after Jesus' birth.

Nicholas grew up in a country we call Turkey. He lived near a part of the ocean called the Mediterranean Sea. You can see it on our map.

When Nicholas was a little boy, he liked to help people. When Nicholas grew up, he continued to help people. "God loves me and cares for me," Nicholas thought, "so

Nicholas was born in Patara, near Myra, on the Mediterranean Sea.

Boys and girls wore clothes like this when Nicholas was growing up.

I want to love and care for people." Nicholas became a pastor of a church. The church was in a city called Myra. In those days, pastors were called bishops. Everyone called Nicholas, "Bishop Nicholas."

GIVING A SURPRISE PRESENT

A poor man lived in Myra. He had three daughters, but he did not have any money. He was in trouble because he could not take care of his girls. What should he do?

Bishop Nicholas heard about the poor man. He wanted to help him. He decided to give the man a present of money. Then the man would be able to care for his daughters. But Nicholas thought, "If I give the man money, he will tell everyone about me.

He will tell people how nice I am." Nicholas said to himself, "I don't want that. God gave me this money. When I give this present, I do not want the man to think about me. I do not want the man to say I was kind. I want him to think about God and thank God for caring for him."

Nicholas thought, "I want this present to be a surprise. I do not want the man to know I gave it to him." Is there a way Nicholas could keep it a surprise? What do you think he did?

Nicholas waited until nighttime when it was pitch black outside. Everyone was asleep. Nobody was watching. Nicholas snuck up to the poor man's house. The man had left a window open. Nicholas crept up to the window. He tossed the bag of money inside. The bag landed beside the fireplace.

The next morning, the poor man woke up and found the money beside his fireplace. "Who put this here?" he wondered. "Some kind person has given this to us!" Then the man thanked God for sending money, so he could care for his daughters.

A BIG ARGUMENT ABOUT GOD

One day, Nicholas heard people in his city arguing about God. They asked, "Is Jesus *really* God? Do we *really* need to love and worship Him? What does the Bible actually say about Jesus?" People all over the Roman and Greek world started arguing like this.

A man named Constantine was ruler of the Roman and Greek world. Constantine wondered, "What should I do? People are arguing. They are saying false things about Jesus." Constantine planned a meeting. He invited hundreds of pastors to come to the meeting. Everyone gathered for the meeting in the city of Nicaea. (The meeting was called a *council*.)

Bishop Nicholas was one of the men who came to the meeting. Constantine

Constantine was emperor of the Roman and Greek world.

waited until all the pastors and guests had arrived. Then he said, "We must believe what the Bible says. Is Jesus God? Does the Bible say so?"

The pastors began to talk about this. They talked for a long time. "The Bible is true, and the Bible tells us that Jesus is God," they said. "We should love Him and worship Him." Then the bishops wrote down what they believed. We call this document they wrote the Nicene Creed. Have you heard of it before? Your mommy or daddy can read it to you.

WHAT HAPPENED LATER?

Nicholas was happy to help write the Nicene Creed. He wanted everyone to love Jesus as much as he did.

After the meeting was over, Nicholas went back to his home in Myra. He lived a long time, until he was an old man. Then he died. People loved Nicholas very much. People wanted to be like Nicholas. After he died, they remembered all the things he had done. Some people remembered the gifts he had given to poor people. They started giving gifts too. If a poor child had no food, someone would wait until the child went to sleep at night. Then they would quietly put food and toys beside the fireplace in the child's house. When the child woke up in the morning, they would find the special presents waiting for them.

Beloved, if God so loved us, we also ought to love one another. (1 John 4:11)

Bishop Nicholas of Myra

DISCUSSION QUESTIONS

1. What kind of clothes did boys and girls wear when Nicholas was a little boy?
2. What did Nicholas do to help the poor man take care of his daughters?
3. Why did Nicholas bring his present to the poor man's house at night?
4. Do you remember what the Nicene Creed is?
5. What does our Bible verse teach us?

Camels in the African desert

A VERY BAD LITTLE BOY: AUGUSTINE AND THE PEAR TREE

5

Long, long ago, a little boy lived in a country we call Algeria. Algeria is in Africa. It is a land full of deserts. Do you know what a desert is? It is a place where no trees grow. No grass grows either. A desert is full of hot, hot sand.

The little boy was born in AD 354. He lived near the desert, but he did not live in the desert. The air was very hot where he lived, but there were still trees and grass nearby. The boy's name was Augustine.

When Augustine was a tiny baby, his mother started praying for him. (His mother's name was Monica.) Monica wanted her son to grow up to be a good man. She wanted him to be a man who loved God. Every day, she prayed that Jesus would take care of her little boy. She prayed He would make him a godly man.

Augustine loved his mother, but he was a naughty child. He did not like to obey. When his mother told him it was time to study his letters, Augustine tried to run away and play. He did not like to do schoolwork.

"I do not want to learn the ABCs!" Augustine complained.

"You must learn them, even if you do not want to," his mother told him.

Augustine sat down and studied like his mother told him to. But he did not like to do his schoolwork. He frowned as he looked at the ABCs he had to learn. Inside, he was not thinking about ABCs. He was thinking about going outside and playing. He was thinking about skipping his schoolwork.

A PEAR TREE AND SOME PIGS

As Augustine got older, he kept doing bad things. One day, he and some other boys went outside to play. They played all day long. When they finished playing, it was getting dark outside. One of the boys said, "Look at that pear tree!"

Augustine saw the tree. It was a big tree near his house, and it was full of yummy pears. The pear tree did not belong to Augustine's family. It belonged to their neighbor. One of the boys said, "Let us steal the pears on that tree! It is dark outside, so no one will see us."

Augustine knew it was wrong to steal the pears. But Augustine wanted to do everything the other boys did. He smiled and said, "I will help." The boys snuck up to the pear tree. Then they picked the pears. Every boy carried as many pears as he could. They were not hungry, so they did not eat the pears. Instead, they took them to a pen where pigs were sleeping.

"We will give the pigs a treat," one of the boys said. Then Augustine and the other boys threw the pears into the pigpen. The pigs were excited and gobbled up all the pears.

When the owner of the pear tree woke up the next morning, he saw what had happened to his tree. "Someone stole my pears!" he exclaimed. He was very angry,

but he did not know who had stolen the pears. He tried to find out, but no one had seen the thieves.

Augustine knew who had stolen the pears. How could he forget? But he did not tell anyone. When he saw how angry the owner was, Augustine laughed. "He will never guess that we stole the pears and fed them to the pigs!" he thought.

Augustine was a very bad boy. He was glad the owner did not see him steal the pears. He was glad his mother did not see him steal either. Did anyone see Augustine steal the pears?

Someone did see him. Who was it? Do you know? It was God. God saw all the bad things Augustine did. Augustine did not know it, but God was watching him every single day.

"Pick Up and Read"

Soon Augustine grew up. Now he was no longer a bad boy. He was a bad man. Augustine knew he was bad, and he thought, "I must stop doing bad things." But he could not stop. No matter how hard he tried, Augustine kept doing bad things. He was a sad man.

One day, Augustine went out into his garden. He lay down on the ground under a tree and started crying. He wanted to be a good man, but he kept doing bad things. "Is it possible to stop doing bad things?" he asked. "I want to love God and be a good man, but I cannot." Augustine cried and cried.

Then—all of a sudden—Augustine heard something. Near the garden, a child was singing. Augustine sat up and listened. The child sang, "Pick up and read; pick up and read."

"Why is the child saying that?" Augustine wondered. Then he got up and walked back to his house. He said to himself, "Maybe I should read something. Maybe a book will help me." Augustine picked up a book to read. Can you guess what the book was?

Augustine crying in the garden

It was the Bible. The book did help Augustine. The Bible is God's Word. The Bible tells us all about Jesus. Augustine could not stop doing bad things, but God could make Augustine stop. Jesus gave Augustine a new heart. All of a sudden, Augustine loved God and wanted to be like Jesus. He stopped doing bad things. He started doing good things. He started to love God with his whole heart.

When Augustine's mother found out what had happened, she was so glad. "God has heard my prayers!" she said. "I prayed for Augustine every day, even when he was a little boy! Look how God has answered my prayers!"

A Very Bad Little Boy: Augustine and the Pear Tree

WHAT HAPPENED LATER?

Augustine spent the rest of his life learning about God. He spent his life telling people about God. He wrote books to help people learn about Jesus. When you get older, you can read some of his books. But the most important book Augustine ever read was the Bible.

Faith comes by hearing, and hearing by the word of God. (Romans 10:17)

DISCUSSION QUESTIONS

1. What hot place did Augustine live next to?
2. What did Augustine do with the pears he stole?
3. Why was Augustine crying in the garden?
4. What does our Bible verse teach us?

Ural Mountains, Russia

STEPHEN OF PERM: A HOME IN THE COLD MOUNTAINS

6

Far, far away from cities and towns is a long line of mountains called the Ural Mountains of Russia. The Urals are tall mountains that stretch up, up, up into the sky. They are covered in beautiful green trees. But when winter comes, the mountains and trees turn white as snow falls and covers everything. They are in a part of Russia called Siberia.

These mountains in Russia get very cold in the winter. Would you like to live there? If you lived on the Ural Mountains, how would you keep warm?

Some animals live in these mountains. God gave them thick fur coats to keep them warm. Elk, bears, wolves, and wolverines all live in the mountains. They don't mind the snow and cold because they have nice, warm coats to protect them.

God gave elk and reindeer thick fur coats to keep them warm in cold winters.

Some people live in the Ural Mountains too. Long, long ago, in the 1340s, a little boy was born in a mountain village called Ustyug. The boy's name was Stephen. Stephen and his family lived on the west side of the mountains. They lived in a town called Perm. Perm is icy cold in winter. How do you think Stephen and his family stayed warm in the cold and snow?

Look at your skin. Is it furry? God did not give people skin with warm fur like animals have. But the people in the mountains are smart. They made fur coats from the animals that lived there. These fur coats made nice, warm clothes for the Russian people to wear.

The animals lived in forests on the mountains. When Stephen was a little boy, he would watch the men from his village go into the forests. These men were hunters. They walked silently through the deep, quiet forests on the mountains. The men hunted animals they could eat for food. Then they saved the animals' fur to make clothes. Stephen was glad to have warm clothes to wear.

When Stephen was still a little boy, he began to learn many skills. Stephen's father

Russian hunters used fur from foxes to make clothes.

taught him how to sing. They sang in church. They sang with other families in the village. And Stephen learned how to read. He liked to read. He read every book he could find in the village. The books in the village were not written in his language. It was not easy to read these books.

What language do you speak? Stephen spoke the Zyrian language. All the people in Perm spoke Zyrian. But there was no alphabet for Zyrian. The Zyrian language had not been written yet. And there were no ABCs for Zyrian so there were no books in Zyrian either. Stephen wondered when someone would make an alphabet for his language.

TIME TO WRITE AN ALPHABET

When Stephen grew older, he left home and went to a special school. He learned about Greek and many other languages at this school. Then he said, "No one has made an alphabet for my language, so I will make one. Then we can have books written in my language." Stephen began working on a new alphabet. It was hard work, but he did not mind. He wanted the people of his village to have books to read.

First, Stephen made letters for his alphabet. Then, he translated the Bible and

This is the alphabet Stephen created for the Zyrian (Old Permic) language.

Does Stephen's alphabet look different from this one?

wrote it in his Zyrian language. No one had done this before. It was not an easy task. Stephen worked hard and finished at last. He took his new alphabet home to the Ural Mountains.

It was quiet in the mountains when Stephen came home. Stephen could hear the wind blowing through the trees. He could hear water rushing over a waterfall into a deep pool below. He could hear birds singing. Stephen smiled. Were the hunters of the village busy hunting animals for food and clothing? "The hunters bring home good things for us", Stephen thought. "But I am bringing home something special today." Stephen felt excited. Today, he would share his new alphabet with his village. He would share the Bible with his people in a language they could read! Stephen's friends would be able to read the Bible on their own!

WHAT HAPPENED LATER?

Stephen spent the rest of his life teaching people about the Bible. He helped people read God's Word in their own language. The people in the Ural Mountains were happy. They learned Stephen's new alphabet. They began learning the sounds for each letter and reading the Bible and other books in their own language! Stephen was glad. God's Word is a special gift. The Bible teaches us what God has done, and it teaches us how we should live and love Him. Stephen wanted everyone to hear this good news. He was glad God had used him to bring such a special gift to the people of the Ural Mountains.

How sweet are Your words to my taste,
Sweeter than honey to my mouth! (Psalm 119:103)

DISCUSSION QUESTIONS

1. What kind of a land did Stephen live in?
2. How did Stephen and his family keep warm in the cold and snow?
3. What did Stephen do so his people could read books?
4. What does our Bible verse tell us about God's Word?

Hans Sachs lived in the town of Nuremberg in Germany.

HANS SACHS THE SHOEMAKER

Do you know what a nightingale is? It is a bird that loves to sing. It sings at night when other birds have gone to sleep. Nightingales live in many countries around the world. Some of them live in Germany. Once upon a time, a little boy lived in Germany. His name was Hans Sachs, and he was born in 1494. When Hans was a boy, he loved to listen to the nightingales singing in the trees. Would you like to hear them sing?

Hans grew up in a town called Nuremberg. He learned to read and write like other children do. One day, his father said, "Hans, I want you to learn more than reading and writing. I want you to learn how to make shoes."

Nightingales live all over the world. They like to sing at night while other birds are sleeping.

Shoemakers use leather, thread, and special tools to make shoes.

Do you wear shoes? Hans wore shoes every day, but he did not know how to make them. His father found a shoemaker in Nuremberg.

"Will you teach my son how to make shoes?" the father asked.

"Yes," said the shoemaker.

So, Hans began to work with the shoemaker. He became an apprentice. An apprentice is someone who learns by working with an expert. Hans watched everything the shoemaker did. Then he learned how to do the same. Hans learned how to cut out pieces of leather and sew them together to make shoes. He learned how to make big shoes for men and little shoes for children. He made heavy boots for farmers and pretty shoes for ladies to wear to church.

As Hans grew older, he became better and better at making shoes. He learned how to use a hammer to pound tiny nails into shoes to make them strong. Have you had a favorite pair of shoes rip or break? Hans learned how to repair shoes. He became skilled at fixing old shoes so they looked like new!

Hans Sachs worked with the shoemaker for many years. When he was old

A shoemaker uses a special ruler to measure the size of a person's foot. Then he finds a shoe that will fit.

enough, he began to travel to other towns to sell shoes. One day, he came back to his hometown. He opened his own workshop where he made shoes to sell. People in Nuremberg came to Hans to buy shoes.

A NIGHTINGALE STARTS SINGING

When he was twenty-four years old, Hans Sachs got married. He and his wife had seven children.

Hans worked in his shoemaker's workshop each day. Do you think his children learned how to help make shoes? When he finished his work for the day, Hans would have supper with his family. Then he would write poems and read them to his family and friends. Hans liked to make shoes. He liked to write poems too.

A shoemaker is also called a cobbler.

One of his poems was about a man named Martin Luther. Have you heard of Martin Luther? He was a man who taught people about God. He was a preacher and a teacher in Germany. Hans Sachs heard about Luther. "This man teaches good things about God," Hans said. Then Hans wrote a poem about him. In his poem, Luther was a nightingale. The nightingale started singing when it was dark, and people heard the bird sing.

"Luther listens to the Bible, and he tells people what it says," Hans explained. "He is like the nightingale that sings a pretty song at night. God's Word is a beautiful song for us to listen to. We should love it and listen to it just like we listen to the birds singing."

Hans wrote many poems. People liked to read his poems. They published them in books so other people could read them too.

While people were reading his books, Hans kept working in his workshop. Over

Hans read his poems to his friends. They liked them so much that people published his poems in books for others to read.

and over, he cut out pieces of leather. He sewed them together. He nailed soles on the bottoms of the shoes. The shoes Hans made were tough and strong.

Hans Sachs grew older and older, but he kept making shoes. Hans had made shoes as a young man. Hans had made shoes as a father. Hans would make shoes as an old man. He worked hard in his workshop. He wanted children and adults to have strong shoes for their feet. People need shoes to wear, and Hans was glad to work hard to make them. Would you like to be a shoemaker?

Hans Sachs

Whatever your hand finds to do, do it with your might. (Ecclesiastes 9:10)

DISCUSSION QUESTIONS

1. What town in Germany did Hans Sachs live in?
2. How did Hans learn how to make shoes?
3. Hans wrote about a nightingale in one of his poems. Do you remember who the nightingale was?
4. Hans liked to work hard and make good shoes. What does our Bible verse tell us about this?

MARIE VIRET AND A BIG, IRON BELL

8

Marie Viret was born in the 1540s. She lived with her family in a city called Lausanne. Do you see it on the map of Switzerland? Lausanne was a town with many houses and many people in it.

Some people in Lausanne were bakers. They baked bread and sold it each day. Mothers came to buy the bread for their children. Some people in Lausanne were tailors. They made clothes for people to wear.

Marie grew up with her mother and father and her sisters in a town called Lausanne.

Marie's daddy was not a baker or a tailor. He was a pastor. His name was Pierre Viret. Pastor Viret preached at the church in Lausanne. Marie listened to her daddy preach. She listened to him read the Bible at home too. Marie knew she should be a good girl and love God. But at times, Marie did bad things instead.

Do you ever want to disobey? Sometimes it is hard to listen and obey, right? It was this way for Marie. Marie had not learned what happens to people when they disobey. In 1550, Marie was three years old. She did not like to listen and obey. She liked to do things she was told not to do.

On the outside of Marie's house was a big, iron bell. The bell was bigger than Marie's head with a heavy piece of iron attached to it. The heavy iron was nailed to the wall of the house and kept the bell from falling. When a visitor came, they pulled a chain to ring the bell. The bell would make a pretty noise, and Marie's mommy or daddy would come to the door. Marie liked to hear the bell ring. Sometimes when no one was watching, she would slip outside and ring the bell. *Ring, ring, ring*, the bell would go. Her mother would come to the door to see who was there.

"Who is it?" Marie's mother wondered each time. But who did she see? She saw Marie!

"Marie, don't play with the bell!" her mother said.

Marie knew she should obey her mother, but she did not want to. When her mother went back inside, Marie started ringing the bell again. She grasped the chain and pulled and pulled. She was only a little girl, but she could pull with all her might and make the bell ring very loudly. Marie smiled as she listened to the beautiful sound of the bell ringing.

Then, one day, Marie heard a loud *crack!* She had pulled so hard that the heavy piece of iron broke! The iron and the big bell fell down on top of Marie and knocked her to the ground.

Marie was frightened and started to cry. The bell had fallen on her head and hurt her. Her mother and father heard her crying and ran outside to see what had happened.

Marie's daddy picked her up in his arms and hugged her. He saw the bell and the heavy piece of iron lying on the ground beside her.

"Marie, this bell and this piece of iron are very heavy," he said. "They might have killed you when you pulled them down. You might have died." Marie's daddy hugged her very tightly. "God kept you safe when the bell fell down. He did not let the bell kill you."

Marie was sorry she had broken the bell. She knew she should not have played with it and pulled on it so much. Do you think she was glad God kept her safe even when she was being bad?

Marie's daddy carried her back inside. She had bruises on her head where the bell hit her, but she did not die. God protected her. Before long, her bruises healed. Marie's daddy wrote a letter to one of his friends. He told them what Marie had done. In his letter he said, "The bell and the piece of iron were massive. They would have killed a grown man, but Providence protected Marie. God kept her safe."

Do you know what Pastor Viret meant when he said *providence*? Providence is a big word. It means that God is our caregiver. He protects everything He created. Pastor Viret knew God was taking care of his little daughter Marie. God loved Marie and took care of her even when Marie was not thinking about God. As Marie grew older, she would learn to love God too.

When Marie Viret was a little girl, people did not use pencils and pens to write with. When they wanted to write a letter, they used a feather called a quill. They dipped the quill feather into ink. Then they used the quill and ink to write their letter.

THE REFORMATION

Marie lived during the 1500s. In the 1500s, something called the Reformation happened. The Reformation was an exciting time. Many people changed how they lived. They began to follow God and love Him. They began to worship God and read the Bible. Their lives changed because of God and His great love. You will learn more about the Reformation when you are older.

Marie's home was always a busy place during the Reformation. People from other towns and countries came to see her father. When they did, Marie and her sisters and mother had to make food to feed the people. Marie learned how to make bread. She learned how to set the table for mealtime. It was hard to find enough food to feed all the people.

Marie helped her mother prepare food for all the guests who came to see her father, Pastor Pierre Viret.

As she grew, Marie learned to help more and more. She kept listening to her daddy read the Bible. As she listened, she learned to trust God and to love Him. Do you think she ever forgot the day when she pulled on the bell and almost died?

WHAT HAPPENED LATER?

When Marie grew up, she got married. She and her husband started a family of their own in 1565. Soon, Marie would be raising her own children and teaching them what was right and wrong. Do you think her children did bad things at times? No matter what happened, Marie always remembered that God made everything. She remembered that He protects and cares for everything He created. That is what we call *providence*.

And my God shall supply all your need according to His riches in glory by Christ Jesus. (Philippians 4:19)

DISCUSSION QUESTIONS

1. What kind of people lived in Lausanne where Marie grew up?
2. What bad thing did Marie do when she was a little girl?
3. What did Marie's daddy tell her?
4. Do you remember what providence means?
5. What does our Bible verse teach us?

Nordingrå, Sweden

GUSTAVUS ADOLPHUS: KING OF THE SWEDES

9

A long time ago, there was a monk who lived in Germany. His name was Martin Luther. The Lord used Martin Luther to teach people about God's grace. Martin Luther started a time we call the Reformation.

The Reformation was a wonderful time in history! God changed many people's hearts. Many people started reading the Bible again. They began to love God and to follow Him. People compared their churches with what the Bible says. They asked, "Does my church teach what the Bible teaches?" Many people saw that their church did not teach what the Bible says.

They learned from the Bible that God forgives our sins. He loves us and forgives us because of His grace! We are saved because of what Jesus Christ did for us. We cannot do anything good enough to get into heaven. When we trust in Jesus, we are saved. It is our faith in God's son, Jesus, that saves us.

There are two exciting facts to remember about the Reformation! First, God's people realized that only the mercy of God and the sacrifice of Jesus Christ could save them. Our works cannot save us. Only Jesus can save us. And second, God's people looked to the Bible to tell them what to believe and how to live. The blessings of the Reformation spread all over Europe. People in Germany, England, France, and Scotland learned what God's Word says.

In the northern part of Europe, there is a country called Sweden. Take a look at the map on the next page. Can you find Sweden?

Martin Luther

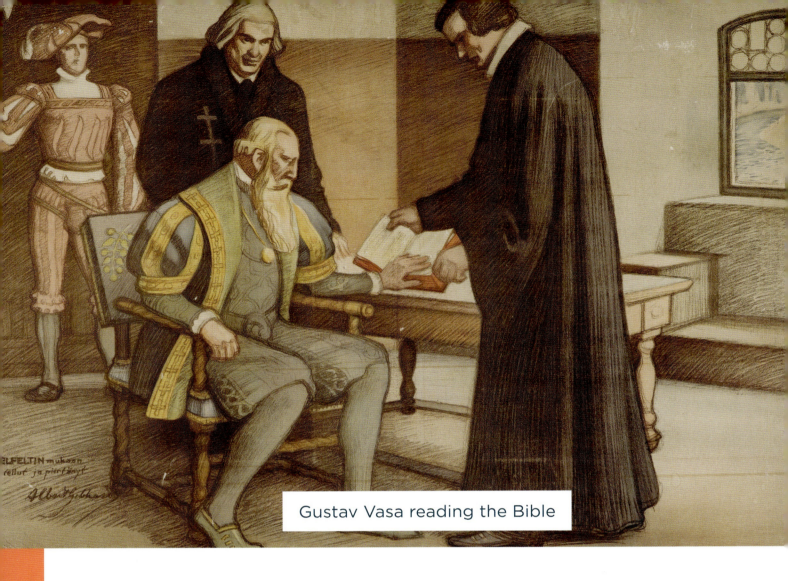

Gustav Vasa reading the Bible

KING GUSTAV VASA

A long time ago, in Sweden, there was a king named Gustav Vasa. He reigned in 1523. This king was special! He led his people to join the Reformation. King Gustav Vasa began to read the Bible. He found that the teaching of the Reformation was true. The king and the Swedes began to follow the Bible.

King Gustav explained what it means to be a Christian. Here is what he said: "To be a Christian is to serve God exactly as His law tells us to. It is to love God more than anything. It is to believe in Jesus Christ as our only Savior. It is to study and teach the Bible. It is to love everyone just as much as we love ourselves."

The king also taught the Swedes to turn away from idols. The king wanted everyone to love God and serve Him. The king saw idolatry in the Roman Catholic church, and he was not happy. He believed that praying to saints was idolatry. And he believed that worshiping the bread and wine of communion was not right.

Location of Sweden

The Bible was translated into Swedish in 1541. The Swedish Bible was called the "Gustav Vasa" Bible. It was called this to honor the king who loved God's Word.

King Gustavus Adolphus

A man by a similar name was born many years and many kings later. Gustavus Adolphus was born in December 1594. He was the son of King Charles IX of Sweden (reigned 1604–1611). Young Gustavus Adolphus grew up in a Christian home. Gustavus knew that Jesus Christ was his Savior. Only Jesus could save Gustavus from his sins.

When Gustavus was little, his father wrote him a letter. King Charles knew that one day, Gustavus would be the king. Charles wanted his son to become a wise king. He wanted him to love God more than anything and to take care of the people well.

In his letter, King Charles wrote this: "Gustavus, above all, fear God. Honor your father and mother. Love your brothers and sisters. Be kind and gentle toward your subjects. Punish the wicked. Love the good. Uphold the law."

Charles taught his son Gustavus to love the Lord, and to read God's Word. He wanted Gustavus to be a man of godly character. One day, Gustavus would have a big responsibility. He would be King of Sweden. He would need wisdom, faith, and love to lead the Swedish people. Charles also taught his son to be honest and generous.

King Charles taught his son well. Gustavus became kind and generous to everyone. Once, when Gustavus was a boy, a peasant brought him a little pony from the island of Oeland. The Swedish man offered the pony as a gift to Gustavus. He said, "I want you to accept the pony as a gift. This is a sign of my love and devotion to you." Gustavus answered, "I am glad to have the horse. But I will pay you for it." Then Gustavus took all the money in his purse and gave it to the peasant. The peasant was amazed by how generous Gustavus was.

King Gustavus Adolphus

Charles began training his son to be king when he was little. He included Gustavus in important meetings. He allowed Gustavus to sit in State Cabinet meetings when he was only ten. Charles also brought his son with him to meet leaders from other nations. Gustavus met leaders from all over Europe. He learned many languages. Soon, he could speak to the leaders in their own language.

Charles taught young Gustavus how to fight and lead armies into battle. He taught Gustavus how to ride a horse. He taught him how to use a sword. Gustavus became a mighty warrior when he grew up. Gustavus needed to be strong. One day, he would ride into battle as king, leading the armies of Sweden.

In 1611, King Charles became sick and feeble. He knew that he was soon to die and be with Christ. He called for his son Gustavus. As the king lay ill in bed, Gustavus bowed before his father. Charles placed his hand on the head of Gustavus and said, "Son, you will soon be king." Gustavus wept.

King Charles IX died on October 30, 1611. Gustavus Adolphus became king of Sweden. He was seventeen years old. The young king of Sweden needed all the skills his father had taught him! He needed to be strong and wise. King Gustavus would lead his people through many difficult times. Sweden would fight many battles in the years to come.

At this time, there was a war in Europe that lasted thirty years! Do you think this is a long time to be at war? We call this the Thirty Years War. Many Catholic and Protestant leaders were unhappy in Europe. Catholic rulers in Europe went to war with Protestant rulers. These battles occurred in Germany and Bohemia.

Catholic leaders in Germany plotted against Sweden too. They wanted to take land from Sweden. King Gustavus knew he needed to defend Sweden and the Protestants. He led the Swedes in battle against the Catholic rulers. Gustavus did not want to fight, but he knew that war is sometimes necessary. He fought to restore peace and to protect Sweden.

King Gustavus was a courageous warrior. He did not stay back in the comfort of his palace! He rode out onto the battlefield. He led his men into danger. The soldiers were inspired by the king's faith. They saw that he was a humble man who loved God. Even during long military journeys, Gustavus studied his Bible. He said, "I fortify myself with meditations upon the Holy Bible."

Gustavus also wanted his men to worship the Lord. He wanted to seek God's blessing daily. Every morning and evening, a worship service was held in the army camp. King Gustavus and his men knelt in prayer. They asked God for His blessing as they went into battle. Do you think the men were scared?

On September 6, 1631, Gustavus led his warriors into battle. We call this the Battle of Breitenfeld. All in a line, Gustavus' army sang the Psalms, as they prepared for battle. Then, Gustavus mounted his horse and rode in front of his men. He said: "We fight for the glory of God and the true gospel. Our great God will strengthen us to conquer! He has brought us across seas and rivers, through fortresses and enemies.

This is why we will attack with courage. Our God is with us. May these words be our rallying cry! With the help of the Almighty, victory will be ours."

Gustavus was right. The Swedes were victorious in battle. They defeated the army of the Catholic rulers.

A year later, Gustavus led his men into battle again. The date was November 6, 1632. The battle was held in the town of Lutzen, Germany. King Gustavus and his men cried out to God once more. They knelt in prayer to God before fighting, asking that He would grant them the victory. They sang hymns, including Martin Luther's hymn, "A Mighty Fortress is our God."

A mighty fortress is our God,
A bulwark never failing…

Did we in our own strength confide,
Our striving would be losing,

King Gustavus Adolphus at Breitenfeld

Were not the right Man on our side,
The Man of God's own choosing.
You ask who that may be?
Christ Jesus, it is he…

As the fog lifted over Lutzen, Gustavus led his men into battle. He led them with this cry: "Now, in the name of God, onward! Jesus, make us fight for the glory of Your holy name."

King Gustavus battled with bravery and sacrifice. In the confusion of battle, he became separated from his men. The king was knocked off his horse and killed by enemy soldiers. But the Swedes went on to victory. 10,000 men died in the battle that day. But this battle, along with others, protected Sweden. It protected parts of Germany too. It kept German land out of the hands of Catholic rulers.

Gustavus Adolphus preserved the truth of the Bible and the gospel in Sweden. God used him in many ways. The king was brave and courageous. He was faithful in his reliance on God. He defended Sweden, fought for peace, and stood strong for God's truth.

Watch, stand fast in the faith, be brave, be strong. Let all that you do be done with love. (1 Corinthians 16:13-14)

DISCUSSION QUESTIONS

1. Who started the Reformation?
2. When was the Bible translated into Swedish?
3. How old was Gustavus Adolphus when he became king?
4. What did Gustavus Adolphus do when someone gave him a pony?
5. Name two ways King Charles IX taught his son to be a good king.

Barley field in Lincolnshire, England

SIR ISAAC NEWTON: SCIENCE FOR GOD'S GLORY

10

On Christmas Day in 1642, a baby boy was born in a town called Woolsthorpe, England. He was small and weak, and he could barely cry. His mother, Hannah, thought he would die. Hannah began to cry. She was sad. She did not want her baby to die. Hannah said to her neighbors, "Pray for my baby. His father is dead and this is my only son."

The baby's father had died just before he was born. His father's name was Isaac. So, Hannah named the baby Isaac. God answered Hannah's prayers and saved baby Isaac. Little Isaac grew bigger and stronger every month. God protected him. Before long, Isaac was a normal little boy! He could run and jump and play. He was not weak and sick but strong and healthy.

When Isaac was three, his mother, Hannah, remarried. She married a pastor named Barnabas Smith. He was over sixty years old, but when he asked to marry Hannah, she said yes. Do you think Isaac felt excited? Perhaps now he would have a father to take care of him!

But Pastor Smith did not want to be a daddy to Isaac. He wanted Hannah to live with him, but not Isaac. Isaac had to live with his grandmother. His grandmother lived in a house a few miles from his parents. But Isaac was sad to not live with his mother. He became angry at his step-father, Barnabas. "He is taking my mother from me", thought Isaac. Isaac became a sad, angry little boy. It took a long time before he forgave his parents and was sorry for his anger.

Do you think it was difficult for Isaac to not live with his parents? Little children should stay with their mommy and daddy. But God had a plan for Isaac. Isaac's grandmother was sweet and kind. She loved Isaac and taught him all about God. She taught him to read the Bible. She taught him to pray every day. And she taught him how to live for God and love Him well. Isaac learned to love his Savior Jesus with his whole heart.

When Isaac grew up, he went to a big school called King's School. King's School was in a town called Grantham. God made Isaac's mind smart. He gave him a special ability to learn many things.

Isaac's life changed when he was thirteen. His step-father, Pastor Smith, died. Isaac's mother went back to the family farm. She called Isaac home to help. Isaac was a big help to his family. He helped with his new little sister and brothers. He helped them to not feel so sad after their daddy died. But with the farm, Isaac was not much help. Isaac let the sheep wander. Isaac forgot to feed the cows. Some days, Isaac forgot the animals and read a book instead.

One day, Isaac was leading a horse up a hill by its bridle. He was reading a book at the same time. Isaac loved to read. He was not thinking about the horse. He was thinking about his book. As Isaac walked up the hill reading his book, the horse decided to escape. The horse slipped out of the bridle and began to run. The horse ran and ran, but Isaac did not notice! Up, up, up he walked holding the bridle. When at last Isaac looked up, he found the horse gone and the bridle empty. The horse had run all the way home.

Isaac was a poor farmer! But he *was* one of the brightest students Henry Stokes, the schoolmaster, had seen. "I think Isaac could be a great scientist!" exclaimed Henry to Isaac's mother one day. "He must go back to school!" Isaac's uncle agreed. "God has made Isaac so smart he can go to Cambridge and become a scientist. God must want him to be a scholar!" Do you know what a scholar is? A scholar studies hard and has a special ability to learn things.

Isaac felt excited. He wanted to go to the University of Cambridge. His mother agreed he should go. But first, he had to learn a lot! Isaac studied hard at King's School in Grantham. He wanted to be a great scholar. At last, in 1661, he was ready to go to Cambridge.

At Cambridge, Isaac learned math, chemistry, astronomy, and the Bible. Isaac loved the Bible most. He loved the Bible so much he learned it better than many pastors. He wrote his thoughts in a notebook. Before long, Isaac had filled many notebooks with his thoughts. Isaac said, "I study the Bible daily. I believe the Bible is God's Word to us. I believe God spoke to us through the men who wrote the Bible."

Do you think Isaac liked mathematics? Oh yes, he was smart and loved math. Isaac knew God made math. This made him love math more. One day his teacher asked him a question. He asked, "what is the purpose of life?" Isaac smiled. "It is to learn about God! We can learn about Him by looking at what He made. He made many beautiful things, and He made us smart, so we can learn about them. I know the biggest mistake scientists make! They are proud. They think they succeed all on their own. But God is the Creator of all things, even success."

Isaac was right! The Bible says we were made to glorify God (1 Corinthians 10:31). Do you know what *glorify* means? It means to worship God and to show others how great He is!

Isaac loved astronomy almost as much as he loved math. Isaac loved to look through telescopes. He could see the beautiful sky God made. He could see the little bright stars. He could see the big white moon. And sometimes, he could see the big round planets far, far away. That is what astronomy means. To study all the things God put in the sky! But Isaac was sad. He was poor. He did not have the money for a telescope. So Isaac made a telescope by hand. Then he studied the planets and comets. He used math to see how they moved. God's creation enthralled Isaac.

Isaac Newton's telescope

The Bible tells us that the heavens shine God's glory!

The heavens declare the glory of God;
And the firmament shows His handiwork. (Psalm 19:1)

God had more plans for Isaac Newton! Isaac became a professor at the University of Cambridge. He taught students how to use numbers to understand the world. Isaac was so smart he invented a new kind of math. We call this math *calculus*. Calculus is a tool we can use. We use calculus to work out tough math problems. Would you like to study calculus one day?

Isaac knew a lot about math, but he did not understand gravity. Isaac wanted to learn about everything God made. Isaac thought and thought about gravity. "What is gravity? Why do things fall to the ground?" Isaac wanted to know.

One day, Isaac was sitting under an apple tree. Suddenly, a juicy red apple fell next to him. Isaac picked up the apple and looked at it. And then he looked way up, up, up to the moon. "How can gravity work with the moon?" thought Isaac. "The moon does not fall! I am glad the moon does not fall! But why does it not fall to earth like this juicy red apple?" Why do *you* think the moon and stars do not fall to earth? Do you have any ideas?

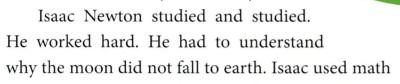

Isaac Newton studied and studied. He worked hard. He had to understand why the moon did not fall to earth. Isaac used math to understand gravity. He used physics too. He wrote a book called *The Mathematical Principles of Natural Philosophy*. Isaac's book is long and hard to read, but it is an important book. Isaac loved God with all his heart. He was happy to work hard to study God's creation. Isaac's book explains how and why things move. It explains God's laws for nature.

The Law of Inertia is the first law Isaac observed. Have you heard of the Law of Inertia? An object will remain at rest until moved by an outside force.

Think of a soccer ball on your lawn. Will the ball move by itself? No! You must kick it with your foot for it to move. Until something pushes on the ball, it will stay in the same place.

Isaac Newton was a great scholar, *and* he was a humble man of God. He knew God made every law of nature. Isaac wrote, "Gravity explains how planets move. But it cannot explain *who* caused them to move. God rules over everything. God knows everything that can or cannot be done. God is the final cause. We know this."

Isaac's hard work helped scientists all over the world. He was one of the most important scientists to live, and one of the smartest men in history. But Isaac knew that he had only learned a little piece of the puzzle of life. There was so much more to know! God knows all things. No matter how much we learn, we cannot know as much as God.

Listen to what Isaac said one day: "I do not know what the world thinks of me.

Isaac Newton when he was 46

But this is how I see myself. I am like a boy playing on a seashore. I am smiling at a pebble! But the whole ocean of truth is in front of me waiting to be discovered."

Isaac Newton died in 1727 at the age of eighty-four. God gave Isaac a long life! He used Isaac to teach many people about the ways of God. Isaac learned a lot about God. He told as many people as he could about God's creation. This is why God made you and me and the whole world! God made us to tell everyone how great God is. We must serve Him with all our hearts!

It is the glory of God to conceal a matter,
But the glory of kings is to search out a matter. (Proverbs 25:2)

DISCUSSION QUESTIONS

1. What happened to Isaac when he was three years old?
2. What did Isaac build so he could look at the planets and stars?
3. Was Isaac a good farmer? Give an example of why or why not.
4. What is the Law of Inertia?

Do you play a musical instrument?

GEORGE FREDERIC HANDEL: MAKING MUSIC AND HELPING CHILDREN

11

Once upon a time, there lived a man who loved music. His name was George Frederic Handel. Handel loved music so much that he played many instruments! Handel played the violin and organ. He played the oboe and harpsichord too.

Do you know what a musician is? Handel was a musician. A musician is someone who plays a musical instrument like a piano or flute or guitar.

Handel was born in 1685. When he was a boy, people dressed different from how they dress today. Men and women wore special wigs to cover their hair. Many men wore white wigs like this man in the picture. They wore long coats with many buttons.

Ladies wore long dresses. Under their dresses were hoops that made the dresses look bigger. Have you ever seen a dress like this before?

When Handel was alive, ladies wore long dresses with hoops that made the dresses look much bigger. Men carried long swords with them.

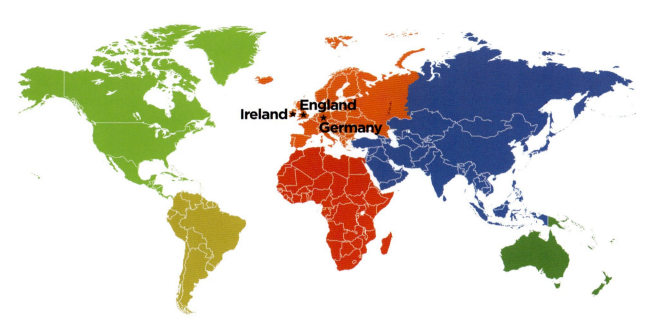

Handel was born in Germany and lived in several countries in Europe. Europe is the orange land on this map.

Handel was born in Germany. When he grew up, he traveled to countries all over Europe. He played music wherever he went. But Handel did not only play music. He wrote music too. Handel was a composer! A composer is a person who writes music. Handel wrote hundreds of pieces of music.

In 1741, Handel went to Ireland. Do you see it on the map? Ireland is a small island near England. Handel had written a special piece of music. He wanted to show it to the people in Ireland. He named his new piece of music, *Messiah*. *Messiah* was a collection of songs and music he wrote about Jesus. It told the story of Jesus' birth and when He lived on earth. It told about the wonderful things Jesus has done for us. Handel used words from the Bible to write his songs. Maybe you can listen to his *Messiah* one day.

Ladies and gentlemen in Ireland came to hear Handel's new music. Handel's *Messiah* amazed them. They loved it! Soon everyone wanted to come hear *Messiah*. But there was a problem. The ladies who came to the performance all wore dresses with hoops. The hoops took up a lot of space. Only a few ladies could fit on the seats inside the building.

The women were not the only problem. In those days, men carried swords with them wherever they went. These long swords took up lots of space! It was difficult for people to squeeze into the building. They needed a lot of room. Nobody could focus on Handel's music. The poking swords and giant hoops were distracting.

Handel had a problem. He could not find room to fit everyone inside, not with all those hoops and swords. But he knew just what to do. He asked all the ladies to leave their hoops at home when they came to listen to the music. "Do not wear hoops under your dresses," he said. "And gentlemen, leave your swords at home too. Then more people will be able to fit inside the building."

Handel's plan worked. The women wore regular dresses without hoops. The men left their swords at home. The building could fit one hundred more people than usual. Handel's *Messiah* music delighted everyone. They came back over and over to listen to it.

An organ is like a piano, but it has more than one keyboard. Some organs have tall pipes behind them.

HELPING THE ORPHANS

Handel went to England after performing in Ireland. He visited an orphanage called the Foundling Hospital. The Foundling Hospital was a home for boys and girls. These boys and girls did not have a mommy or daddy. Handel's heart filled with love for the children. Handel felt sad for them. He wanted to help the boys and girls. What do you think he did? He gave another performance of his *Messiah* music.

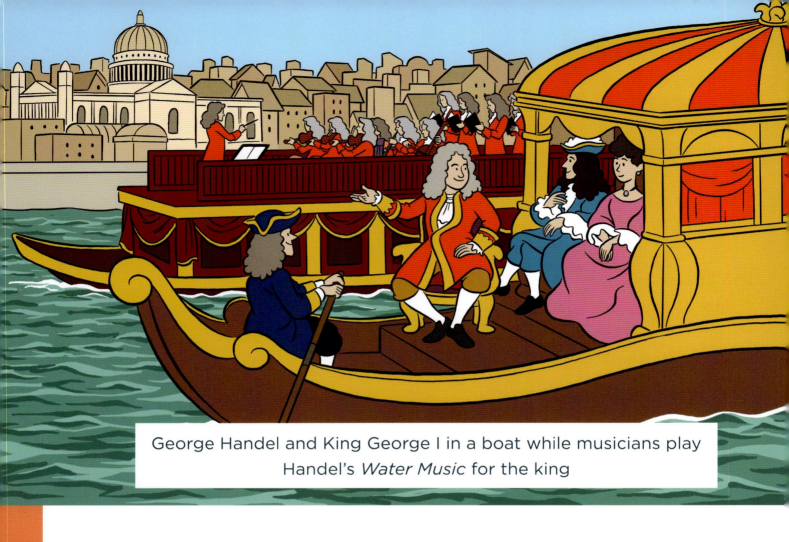

George Handel and King George I in a boat while musicians play Handel's *Water Music* for the king

People in England bought tickets to come hear Handel's music. The tickets cost money. Handel gathered all the money he earned from the tickets. It was a lot of money! What do you think Handel did with it? He gave it all to the orphanage to help the children.

Then he bought an organ and gave that to the orphanage too. Do you think the children liked to listen to the beautiful organ music? Would you like to listen to it?

Handel wrote music for his whole life. He wrote special pieces of music for church. He wrote songs for peo-

George Frederic Handel

ple to sing. He even wrote music for King George I. King George I was the king of England. King George wanted to have a concert while sailing on the Thames River in London. Can you guess what Handel did? He wrote something called the *Water Music*. King George got in his boat. All the musicians climbed into another boat. Then the musicians played music while they were sailing on the river. Do you think it would be fun to sail in a boat and listen to music?

Handel was a good musician and a good composer. He loved to make music that made people happy. Everyone loved to hear his music. They liked to listen to it while he was alive. And they like to listen to it today, hundreds of years later. Handel's music was a great gift to the world!

Rejoice in the LORD, O you righteous!
For praise from the upright is beautiful.
Praise the LORD with the harp;
Make melody to Him with an instrument of ten strings.
Sing to Him a new song;
Play skillfully with a shout of joy.
(Psalm 33:1-3)

DISCUSSION QUESTIONS

1. What kind of clothes did people wear when Handel was alive?
2. What kind of music did Handel write?
3. When people came to hear Handel's *Messiah*, how did they all fit inside the building?
4. What did Handel do with the money he earned from *Messiah* performed in England?
5. What does our Bible verse tell us about playing music and singing?

Waterfalls in India

RAJANAIKEN FINDS A VERY SPECIAL BOOK 12

Have you been to India? India is a beautiful land. India has tall trees and thick forests called rainforests. In these forests are many wild animals. You might see monkeys climbing in the trees, looking for something to eat. Or you might find a tiger. Be careful that the tiger does not eat you!

Long ago, around the year 1702, a child was born in India. His name was Rajanaiken. Rajanaiken lived near Thanjavur, a city in India. When he was a little boy, do you think he liked to watch the monkeys playing in the trees? Do you think he was afraid to go into the rainforest? Tigers can be scary!

As Rajanaiken grew, he learned to read. He loved to read so much that he read many books. He read books written in Tamil. Tamil was the language that people spoke in that part of India.

Rajanaiken grew into a young man. His love for reading continued. One day, someone gave him a book with stories in it. In the book was a story about Jesus. Rajanaiken read the story. Then he said, "Who is this Jesus? I want to learn more about Him."

Rajanaiken tried to find more books about Jesus, but he could not find any. Books were hard to find in India. But Rajanaiken could not stop thinking about Jesus. "Did Jesus *really* come down from heaven to rescue people like me?" he wondered. Rajanaiken wondered what Jesus thought about him. Was Jesus angry with him? He tried to do good things, but he knew he did bad things. This was sin. When Rajanaiken

thought about his sin, he was afraid.

Rajanaiken thought and thought. "I am scared," he said to himself. "I do bad things, and I know God hates sin. What will God do to me? Will God punish me because of all my sins?"

FINDING A BOOK

Rajanaiken wondered and wondered. Then he met a man. The man had a book. Rajanaiken got excited. "Please let me read that book," he said. But the man shook his head. "You cannot have it," he said. The man did not know how to read, but he did not want anyone to have his book.

Rajanaiken looked at the book. The book was in Tamil, his own language. "I know how to read," he said. "Please let me borrow your book." But the man shook his head, "No".

Then Rajanaiken came up with a plan. He did not have any money, but he did have a turban. A turban is a long piece of cloth that people in India use as a hat. "I will give you this turban if you let me borrow your book for a few days," Rajanaiken said. The man smiled. "I will trade with you for your turban," he said. "Give me the turban, and I will let you read my book."

Rajanaiken took the book and started to read. He read all day. When light waned that night, he lit a candle and kept reading. He read for many, many hours while everyone slept. On the next day, he kept reading. He did not know what the book was, but it was excellent. It was the best book he had read in his life. It told him all about Jesus. Do you know what the book was? It was the Bible.

When Rajanaiken finished reading, he knew about Jesus. He began to love Jesus, and he wanted to know more about Him. But then he thought, "When the man comes back for his book, I will not be able to read about Jesus anymore. I must do something!"

Rajanaiken decided that he would write out a copy of the Bible. Then he could keep it after he gave the book back to the man. Rajanaiken did not have any paper. But Rajanaiken was smart. He took leaves from a palm tree and used them as paper. Carefully, he began to copy the words of the Bible. He worked slowly. It was difficult to write all those words. He wanted every word to be perfect. Rajanaiken's hand

became tired from writing. Would you get tired if you wrote every word in the Bible?

Rajanaiken wrote and wrote. In no time at all, his hand was so tired that he could not write. He had to rest before he could write more of God's Word. For days and days he wrote. It was hard work, but he wanted to have a Bible all for himself.

WHAT HAPPENED LATER?

God put so much love in Rajanaiken's heart that he began to tell his friends about Him. He told them about Jesus. His friends did not know how to read, so Rajanaiken read the Bible to them. "I am a sinner," he told his friends. "And you are sinners. You do bad things, and you think bad thoughts. But God saves us from our sin." With God's love, Rajanaiken was no longer afraid. He was happy at last. In 1732, he wrote a letter to tell people what had happened to him. He wrote:

"I am a sinner. But God had mercy on me, and He saved me through His Son Jesus. I will praise our Lord Jesus Christ forever and ever!"

Rajanaiken was thankful that God had given him a Bible. The Bible is a precious gift for us all.

Whenever I am afraid, I will trust in You. In God (I will praise His word), in God I have put my trust....
(Psalm 56:3-4)

DISCUSSION QUESTIONS

1. If you went to India, what kinds of animals might you see in the rainforest?
2. Why was Rajanaiken scared when he thought about his sin?
3. What did Rajanaiken do with the Bible he read?
4. What does our Bible verse teach us today?

Mountains in Ladakh Region, India

Girls in Persia wore head coverings like this one.

13
KHANEE AND THE NEW SHOES

Khanee was a little girl who lived in Persia. She was born in 1832. Today, we call Persia *Iran*. Iran is a desert country with lots of hot sand and only a few trees.

When Khanee was ten, she started going to school every day with other young girls. Some of the girls were older, and some of the girls were younger. They were all friends and went to school together. The girls had an American teacher. Her name was Fidelia Fiske.

Miss Fiske taught the Persian girls how to read and write. She was a wonderful lady, and the girls loved her. Miss Fiske was kind and gentle. This surprised Khanee. Khanee did not like to be kind and gentle. She liked to do bad things and call people

Khanee grew up in Persia. Today, Persia is called Iran.

names. Nobody could look inside Khanee and see her heart. But if they could, they would have seen a lot of bad things.

If Khanee was angry with one of the girls, she would say, "You silly buffalo!" It was not nice to call someone a buffalo, but Khanee did not care.

One day, Khanee decided to do something naughty. One of the girls at school named Sawdee had gotten a new pair of shoes. The shoes were beautiful, and everyone liked them. When Sawdee came inside, she set her shoes down beside the door. Khanee waited until no one was watching. Then she snatched the shoes and rushed outside. In the schoolyard was a well. A well is a deep hole with water in it. Khanee looked around to be sure no one saw her. Then she threw the shoes into the well. They sank down, down,

Sawdee loved her beautiful new shoes.

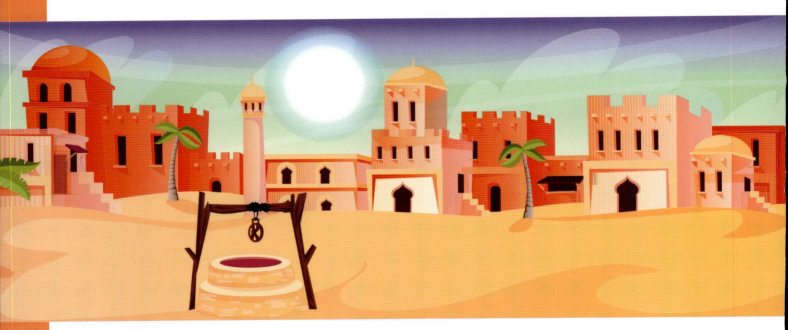

Persia is full of deserts. There is little water, so people dig wells to get water. A well is a deep, deep hole with water at the bottom. People lower a bucket on a rope and fill it with the water in the well. Then they pull the bucket back up so they can drink the water.

down into the water and disappeared. Then Khanee went back into the schoolroom and pretended nothing had happened.

Sawdee was heartbroken when she could not find her shoes. She loved those pretty shoes. All the girls helped her look for them. Miss Fiske helped search for the shoes too.

"Where could they be?" Sawdee cried. "I know I left them right here!"

"Someone must have stolen them," Miss Fiske said with a sigh. "Perhaps a stranger took them when we were doing our schoolwork. Maybe he stole them while we were reading."

Everyone wondered who had stolen the shoes. Everyone but Khanee. Khanee smiled to herself. "They will never find out who took them!" she thought.

GOD CHANGES KHANEE

Miss Fiske read the Bible to the girls each day at school. She knew the girls had sin in their hearts. She prayed and asked God to give the girls new hearts that would love Him and love each other. Khanee and the other girls listened to Miss Fiske read, but they did not change. They still did bad things and called each other bad names.

God saw what the girls were doing. He saw their bad hearts. He knew they were naughty children. What do you think He did? One day, as the girls were in school, God began to give them new hearts. All of a sudden, the girls realized they were doing bad things. They became very sorry and prayed to Jesus.

Khanee was sad when she thought about the bad thing she did to Sawdee's new shoes.

Khanee used to be happy when she did bad things. But God changed her heart. Now, she began to feel sad when she called someone a bad name. She started to cry. Then she prayed and asked God to forgive her.

Miss Fiske explained that God forgives sins. He sent Jesus to die on the cross and save His people from their sins. Khanee smiled when she heard this good news. She began to love Jesus and want to follow Him.

At first, Khanee was happy. She began to read the Bible by herself, and she liked to pray to God and sing to Him. But then she started thinking about all the bad things she had done. She thought about Sawdee's new shoes that she had thrown into the well.

"What should I do?" Khanee wondered. Then she knew what she had to do.

Miss Fiske was in her room when she heard a knock on the door. It was Khanee.

"What is it, Khanee?" Miss Fiske asked.

Khanee started to cry. "I did something terrible," she said. "Do you remember when Sawdee got her new shoes?"

"Yes," Miss Fiske said. "Someone stole the shoes, and Sawdee was heartbroken."

"I stole the shoes," Khanee said quietly. "A stranger didn't take them; I did. I stole them and threw them in the well so nobody would find them."

Miss Fiske was surprised. "Khanee, that was a terrible thing to do," she said.

"Yes, it was. I was a naughty girl. But now I know that Jesus wants me to confess my sins. He wants me to tell you what I did, and then He wants me to fix the bad things I did."

"What do you mean?" Miss Fiske asked.

"I have to tell Sawdee that I stole her shoes," Khanee explained. "But I have to do more than that. I want to work and earn money, so I can buy her a new pair of shoes. Is that the right thing to do?"

Miss Fiske smiled. "Yes, that is an excellent thing to do," she said.

Khanee worked hard to earn money to pay for the shoes. She was

Fidelia Fiske was Khanee's teacher.

no longer an angry little girl. She was happy and smiling all the time. Miss Fiske smiled every time she saw Khanee. "Khanee, you are just like a bright and shining light in our school," she said. "Jesus has changed your heart."

WHAT HAPPENED LATER?

Khanee was a very happy girl. Later on, she grew into a very happy woman. She got married and had children of her own. Sometimes her life was easy, and sometimes it was hard. But whatever happened, she knew that Jesus loved her. "I want to be faithful," she told her friends. "I want to love Jesus all my life long."

For God so loved the world that He gave His only begotten Son, that whoever believes in Him should not perish but have everlasting life. (John 3:16)

Let him who stole steal no longer, but rather let him labor, working with his hands what is good, that he may have something to give him who has need. (Ephesians 4:28)

DISCUSSION QUESTIONS

1. What was the name of Khanee's teacher?
2. What did Khanee do with the shoes she stole?
3. When God gave Khanee a new heart, what did Khanee do?
4. Why did Khanee want to pay for the shoes she had stolen?
5. What do our Bible verses teach us?

Puaaiki was born on this island called Maui.

BARTIMAEUS PUAAIKI, THE BLIND BOY OF HAWAII

14

On a string of islands in the middle of the Pacific Ocean lives a group of people. We call these people the Hawaiians. And we call their islands Hawaii. The Hawaiian Islands are filled with beauty. There are green plants and tall trees. They are full of flowers too! There are volcanoes that can shoot fire into the sky in Hawaii. Would you like to see a volcano?

On one of these islands, a little boy was born in 1785. When his mommy saw the child, she said, "I don't want to keep this little boy." She did not want any children. What do you think happened to the baby? God was looking out for him! Another

Maui is part of a group of islands called the Hawaiian Islands.

mother saw him and said, "I love you. I will take care of the you." So she took the little boy and kept him safe. She named him Puaaiki.

Puaaiki grew up on an island called Maui. He liked to run and play with the other little boys on the island. They played in the rainforests and on the beaches. They even played in the waves in the ocean. But they were careful with sharks. Many sharks lived in the ocean near Puaaiki's home. The people on the island believed the sharks were gods. They brought offerings to the sharks and prayed to them. Puaaiki did this too. He did not know how silly it was to think a shark was a god. He did not know who the true God was because he had not heard about Jesus.

Puaaiki was a bad boy. He learned to do many bad things as he was growing up. Like all of us, Puaaiki needed a Savior. But Puaaiki didn't know this yet.

Sometimes, God uses hard things in our life so that we will look to God for help. A hard thing happened to Puaaiki. One day he got sick. The sickness hurt his eyes, and he became blind. Puaaiki could see nothing. He could not see the other boys running and playing. He could not see the pretty flowers or trees on the island. He could not see the waves in the ocean or watch them crashing against the shore.

Puaaiki was a sad boy. He grew up and became a man, but he was still blind, and he was still sad. One day, a little boy saw him. "Why are you sad?" the boy asked. "I have good news for you. Come with me, and you can hear the good news." Puaaiki could not walk by himself because he could not see his steps. He might run into something or fall down and hurt himself. So the boy took Puaaiki's hand and led him to a preacher. A man from the United States had come to Hawaii. He had come to teach the Hawaiians about Jesus.

Puaaiki listened to the man speak. The man told him that God created the whole world. He created the little island where Puaaiki lived. God created Puaaiki too. God took care of Puaaiki when he was a little baby and his mother did not want him. And God took care of Puaaiki when he became blind. He helped him when he could not see. When Puaaiki heard this, he began to love God. "Now I know that the shark is not a true god," he said. "Now I love Jesus Christ, and I want to do what He tells me to do."

Puaaiki began to change. He did not want to do bad things. He wanted to love

Now Puaaiki knew that the shark god was not a real god at all.

God and not love sin. There were other people on the Hawaiian Islands who loved God. They were happy when Puaaiki began to love God. The Christians baptized him. Then Puaaiki changed his name. He wanted everyone to know that Jesus had changed his heart. His name would not be Puaaiki. His name would be Bartimaeus.

Joy filled Bartimaeus Puaaiki. He wanted to tell everyone about God and His great love! He wanted everyone to know that Jesus was the real God. The shark god was not real at all.

WHAT HAPPENED LATER?

Bartimaeus Puaaiki loved Jesus. He wanted to do everything that pleased Jesus. Though he was blind, he began to take care of his family. He planted a garden. He grew potatoes and bananas so his family would have food to eat. He talked to other fathers and mothers. He told them they should take care of their children. He told them, "If you lose your hat, won't you look around until you find it? You are very careful with your hat. But you should be even more careful with your children. You need to

Bartimaeus worked hard to grow bananas and other food to feed his family.

take care of them and teach them the good Word of God. This is the most important thing you can do for them."

Bartimaeus loved God, and he spent the rest of his life living for Jesus.

Grave marker of Bartimaeus Puaaiki

For none of us lives to himself, and no one dies to himself. For if we live, we live to the Lord.... (Romans 14:7-8)

DISCUSSION QUESTIONS

1. When Puaaiki was a little boy, what animal did he worship?
2. Who helped Puaaiki learn the good news about Jesus?
3. After Puaaiki became a Christian, why did he plant a garden?
4. What does our Bible verse tell us about how we should live?

When Puaaiki picked a new name, he wanted to be called Bartimaeus. Why do you think he picked that name? Long ago, when Jesus lived on Earth, a blind man named Bartimaeus asked Jesus to heal him. Jesus did heal him, and the blind man could see again. Puaaiki wanted everyone to call him Bartimaeus just like the man Jesus healed. He said, "Jesus gave that man new eyes so he could see, and Jesus gave me a new heart to love Him!" You can learn more about the Bartimaeus in the Bible if you ask someone to read you Mark 10:46-52.

Hand-tapping morse code on a telegraph machine

SAMUEL MORSE: ARTIST AND INVENTOR

15

Talking to people far away is easy. Have you ever used your parent's phone? You can dial a number and talk to people all over the world!

We can even *see* someone's face on a video call. That person could be down the street or across an ocean. We can talk to anyone anywhere with the click of a button. We do not need to wait for a letter to arrive in the mail. What a wonderful gift we have with our fast, easy messaging.

But in the past, it was not this easy to talk to people far away. Can you imagine waiting weeks or months to hear from your friend? Imagine if a man living in England wanted to send a letter to his friend in America. A mailman would place the letter on a ship. The ship would sail across the Atlantic Ocean. It would take a month or more to cross the ocean. Another mailman would carry the letter over land. It would take a week or more to travel over land. Finally, the man's friend would receive the letter. But then it would take many more weeks for his reply to travel back to England.

Would you like to wait forty or fifty days to get a letter from your friend? This seems like a long time to us. A lot can happen in forty or fifty days.

Samuel F.B. Morse (1791–1872) knew that this was a problem. He wished that messages could reach people faster.

Samuel grew up in America during the War of 1812 with England. In December 1814, England signed a peace treaty. Do you know what a peace treaty is? A peace treaty ends a war. But news traveled slowly. Six weeks before news reached America, a battle began. The war was over, but the men kept fighting. They fought the Battle of New Orleans in January of 1815. Many lives were lost because of slow communication.

A mailman on horse

Samuel watched this sad event happen. He wished messages could be sent faster. But how could he solve the problem? The Lord would give Samuel wisdom one day to solve this problem. He would put an idea in Samuel's head. One day, Samuel would create an amazing invention called the *telegraph*. His invention would change the world.

Who was Samuel Morse, and what did he do before he built the telegraph? Samuel was not always a world-famous inventor. First, he was a famous artist. He painted pictures and made sculptures for important people.

Samuel grew up in Boston with his family. When Samuel was little, he loved to draw and paint. He liked to see the paints fill the paper with bright color and feel the weight of the brush in his hand. Samuel liked to draw beautiful pictures for his family and friends too. He liked to make people happy with his art. How do you think he became a famous artist? Do you think it was easy?

No, it was not easy to become a famous artist in Boston! Samuel's father was a pastor named Jedidiah Morse. Jedidiah was very wise. He liked Samuel's art, but he did not want him to become an artist. Artists did not make much money. How would Samuel earn a living and support a family as an artist?

Samuel listened to his father. He wanted to make a good living and have a big family. But as he grew up, his talent could not be hidden. Pastor Morse looked at his son's paintings and said, "God has given you this gift, Samuel! You must honor God with this gift of art." So Samuel continued to paint and draw. And his family supported him. They told him, "You will make many people happy with your paintings! Use your skill to serve the Lord!"

When Samuel grew up, he moved to the big city of London. He lived in London for four years during the War of 1812. Why did Samuel live in London? He wanted to learn from an artist called Benjamin West. The whole world knew about Benjamin's art! He was an excellent painter. Before long, Samuel became an excellent painter too. When he returned home to America, he could paint beautiful portraits of people. There were few artists who could paint as well as Samuel. His years of practice paid off.

But Samuel still worried. "How will I make enough money to care for a family?" he wondered. "And where can I find people who will buy my portraits?" Painted portraits were not cheap. Only people with lots of money could buy them. Samuel

Samuel Morse's studio in Charleston, South Carolina

thought and thought. Then he had an idea. Maybe people in South Carolina would pay for his portraits! So, Samuel traveled to Charleston, South Carolina. There were many wealthy people in Charleston. They were happy to pay Samuel for his portraits. In no time at all, he had many customers. His reputation grew and grew.

Can you guess whose portraits Samuel painted? Samuel was so talented he was asked to paint President James Monroe. He spent weeks in the White House, working on President Monroe's portrait. He wanted it to be perfect! And he painted other famous portraits too. He painted portraits for President John Adams, Eli Whitney, and the Marquis de Lafayette.

Portrait of James Monroe

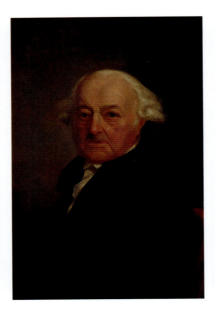
Portrait of John Adams

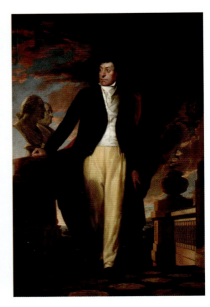
Portrait of the Marquis de Lafayette

Take a look at some of Samuel's excellent paintings!

In 1818, God gave Samuel a special gift. God gave him a wife. Her name was Lucretia Walker, and she was sweet and kind. Everyone loved Lucretia. She was good at making people feel welcome. She loved God very much too. Samuel and Lucretia were very happy together. They made many plans for the future. They wanted to have lots of children. Soon their dream began to come true, and they had three little children. They wanted to grow old together, have many more children, and raise their big family to love God.

Then, something awful happened. One day, when Samuel was on a business trip, Lucretia had a heart attack. Samuel's father wrote a letter to him at once. But it was too late. Lucretia had died and Samuel would never see her again. Samuel cried and cried. He was heartbroken. "How could this happen?" he wondered. "If only I had gotten the message right away! If only I could have been home for Lucretia's death! What if the news had reached me when there was still time?"

Samuel's heart was broken, but he trusted God. "God will give me the strength for this," he thought. "Maybe with God's help I can solve this problem. Maybe I can solve this problem of slow communication."

Two things had fascinated Samuel since he was a boy. Do you know what they were? Art and electricity. Do you think God could use both art and electricity to make a new invention? Samuel thought and thought about electricity. "What is it for?" he wondered. "How can it be used to help people?"

Then, in 1832, God gave Samuel a brilliant idea. Samuel was returning home from France to New York on a big boat named *Sully*. One day, he was relaxing on the deck with a friend named Dr. Charles Jackson. Dr. Jackson was a scientist. He began to tell Samuel about electricity. Samuel listened carefully. He loved to hear about electricity. "Benjamin Franklin passed an electric current through many miles of wire," Dr. Jackson said. "He noticed that a touch at one end caused a spark at the other. There was no difference of time between touch and spark. It was instant."

All of a sudden, Samuel had an idea. What if messages could be instant too? What if electricity could be used to send them? Maybe an electric signal could be sent over many miles! Samuel began to work on his idea. He worked hard. He worked late into the night. He worked early in the morning. He drew and drew and drew. Soon his notebook was filled with sketches of his idea.

Samuel created a code language too. Do you know what the code was? It was made of little dots and dashes. Different combinations of dots and dashes made different letters. The letters could be strung together to form words and sentences. The code was very useful. It could be sent over a special wire to create a message.

Samuel worked on his idea for twelve years. He worked and worked and worked. He taught art too. Samuel was a good art teacher. He did not make much money, but he loved art so much he did not care. Some weeks he had to skip meals, but he kept working on his idea. Despite these challenges, Samuel kept working on his telegraph. He believed his idea could work.

Then one day, Samuel showed his telegraph to a group of people. These people were scientists and government officials. Do you think they liked Samuel's invention? No! They laughed at him. "What a silly idea!" they said. "How can messages be sent through 'electricity'? Messages can never be sent over long distances." The telegraph seemed silly to them because it had never been tried.

But Samuel wanted to help people with his telegraph, so he kept working. He knew that God made electricity as a gift. He knew God would be happy to see His gift used well! Samuel once said: "I believe God created the great forces of nature. This was to show His infinite power. But God also made these forces of nature to show His

good will to man. God created the forces of nature for the benefit of mankind. We must discover how to use them."

At long last, after twelve years, God blessed Samuel's invention. The American Congress said, "We will provide money for your project, Samuel. We think your telegraph idea will work." An electric line was stretched all the way from Washington, D.C. to Baltimore. Do you know how long that is? That is over 38 miles (61km)!

May 24, 1844, was a big day. The time had come to test the telegraph line. The first telegraph machine was placed in the basement of the Supreme Court building. Everyone in Washington, D.C., (where the Supreme Court is), held their breath. The people in the railway station in Baltimore held their breath too. That is where the second machine was placed. Would they get the message from the Supreme Court? Samuel could hardly wait to see.

Henry Ellsworth's daughter, Annie, was chosen to pick the first message. Henry was the U.S. Patent Commissioner. The message was short and simple. "What hath God wrought," she penned. The phrase comes from the Bible in Numbers 23:23.

Samuel Morse: Artist and Inventor

Original telegraph message: "What hath God wrought"

Samuel sat down at the telegraph machine. This was a big moment. Slowly, he began to tap that first message. *Tap, tap, tap* went his fingers in Morse code. Alfred Vail in Baltimore waited. He bit his lip. Would the telegraph work? Then, all of a sudden, Alfred saw something. He saw a dot, and a dash, and then another and another and another. He shouted with joy. He sent the same message back to Samuel. Samuel tore off the ribbon paper and held it high for all to see. Everyone began to clap. Samuel's idea had worked! They laughed and cheered with joy.

Samuel said, "Annie Ellsworth's sentence was divinely inspired. It will be in my thoughts day and night. 'What hath God wrought!' What good things God has given us! This is His work. He alone carried me through all my trials. He gave me strength

Washington, D.C., to Baltimore

to overcome obstacles. 'Not unto us, not unto us, but to Thy name, O Lord, be all the praise.' "

Samuel's idea changed the world. Before long, telegraph lines stretched all over America. New jobs were created in cities and villages. People were trained to send messages by telegraph. They were trained to use the special language called Morse code. The telegraph changed lives everywhere. It made hundreds of thousands of people happy. At last, people did not need to wait to hear from each other.

Samuel Morse in 1866

WHAT HAPPENED LATER?

Years later, in 1871, a statue of Samuel Morse was built. It was built in Central Park, New York City. Samuel was alive for the revealing of his own statue. But he was a humble man and did not attend. He did not want to be improper. "How can I cheer for my own statue?" he wondered. But everyone wanted to meet Samuel. So he attended the reception held afterward. Thousands of other telegraph operators attended the reception. They all wanted to shake Samuel's hand. They could not wait to meet the famous inventor, Samuel Morse.

A telegraph machine was set up at the reception hall. Samuel was invited to send a final message. The message would be read by stations all across America. This would be Samuel's farewell message to the world. What did Samuel Morse choose to tell the U.S. and Canada? Here is his final message through Morse code:

"Greetings and thanks to the telegraph fraternity throughout the world. Glory to God in the highest, on earth peace, good will to men. S.F.B. Morse."

Samuel Morse knew what life was all about: bringing glory to God. He did not live for himself. He lived for the Lord. Samuel did exactly what Psalm 115 tells us to do:

Not unto us, O Lord, not unto us,
But to Your name give glory,
Because of Your mercy,
Because of Your truth. (Psalm 115:1)

DISCUSSION QUESTIONS

1. Before Samuel Morse invented the telegraph, what was his job?
2. What message did Samuel Morse send through the telegraph in 1844?
3. Where did Samuel's message get sent to in 1844?
4. What does our Bible verse teach us?

Fall in Ontario, Canada

BETTY MOVES TO A NEW HOME

Betty Schneider was born in 1802. Her family were Germans. They had moved from Germany many years before Betty was born. They lived on a farm in Pennsylvania now. Betty lived in a small house with her family. She had a father and mother and seven brothers and sisters.

One day, when Betty was four years old, her father, Jacob, came home with exciting news. He said, "Children, we are going to move to a new home. We will have a new house and a new farm. We're going to a country called Canada."

Betty wondered what Canada was like. What would her new home look like? Would it be the same as her old home? Would she like to live in Canada?

Betty's mother, Mary, began to pack. She packed all the clothes and all the blankets in their house. Then she packed the cups and plates. Betty's older sisters Anna and Polly helped pack. Betty wanted to help too. Do you think she was big enough to fold the heavy blankets? Do you think she needed help to lift them?

Betty's father bought two big wagons. The wagons had thick cloth coverings for roofs. Betty's father and older brothers, Christian and Jacob, loaded everything into the wagons. Betty wanted to watch. She stretched as tall

When Betty Schneider was born, girls wore clothes like this.

Do you think Betty helped pack the food they would need for their long trip?

as she could, but she was too little to see inside the wagon. Her father picked her up and put her inside.

"What do you think, Betty?" he asked. "Will this be a nice home for us while we travel to Canada?"

"Oh yes!" said Betty.

"It will take us a long time to get there," her father said. "We'll travel for more than four weeks. That's four Sundays and all the days in between."

When everything was packed, Betty's family climbed into the wagons. Other families came with them. Each family had their own wagon to ride in. The wagons were like little houses that traveled on wheels. Betty's father and older brothers showed the horses which way to go.

The wagon creaked and rattled as Betty rode inside it. She watched as they rolled past fields and forests. The cows from their farm came with them on the journey. Betty's daddy worked hard to keep all the cows together. He did not want them to get lost on the long trip.

Betty rode in a covered wagon like this. Would you like to ride in one?

The wagons traveled all day long. When it was almost nighttime, Betty's father stopped the wagon, and everyone got out to help gather wood for a fire. Betty's mother cooked soup over the fire. Then it was time to sleep. Betty's mother and older sisters, Anna and Polly, spread out blankets in the wagon for beds.

Betty curled up in one of the blankets. She had never slept outside before. She could hear the horses munching grass near the wagon. Somewhere close by, she could

Betty's family milked their cows and had milk and butter on their long journey.

hear crickets singing. Farther away, she heard her daddy talking to the other men. They were making plans for the next day. Betty sat up and looked out the back of the wagon. High above her, the stars were twinkling in the night sky.

"Lie down, Betty," her mother said softly. "It's bedtime."

Betty snuggled back into her blanket and listened as the crickets kept singing. Soon she was fast asleep.

CROSSING A WIDE RIVER

Days and days passed as Betty's family traveled with their wagons. "Will we ever reach Canada?" Betty wondered.

One day, they came to a big river called the Susquehanna. There were no boats or bridges to carry them across the river.

"We're stuck!" thought Betty. "Now we'll have to go back home again."

Betty and her family had to find a way across the Susquehanna River to reach Canada.

Covered wagons often crossed rivers because there were no bridges they could use.

But her father knew what to do. He carefully led the horses into the river. The big wagon wheels went down into the water. "We'll ride across," said her father. "The wagon will carry us."

Betty watched as the water climbed higher and higher around the wagon. Soon it had almost covered the wheels. Do you think Betty got scared?

Betty's father led the horses farther into the river. The water was so high that some of it started splashing into the wagon where Betty was sitting.

"Help!" cried Betty. "The water will wash us away!"

Betty felt scared. She wanted to go home. She did not want to go to Canada anymore. But her mother said, "Betty, your daddy will take care of us. He knows how to get across the river."

Slowly, the wagon moved across the river. More water splashed into the wagon. Betty's blanket got wet, and she began to cry. But Betty's father brought them safely across the river.

At last, both wagons made it all the way across the river. Betty was happy to be on the other shore. Her older brothers and sisters took all the wet things out of the wagon. They hung them in the hot sun to dry.

Betty was still a little scared, but her father picked her up in his strong arms. He smiled. "Don't worry, Betty," he said. "God kept us safe, didn't He? We must thank Him for taking care of us. God takes good care of us when we're scared."

Betty had forgotten that God was watching over them. She had forgotten that God was stronger than the river. He could keep them safe, and He did.

Betty and her family moved to Canada and lived near Hamilton in Ontario.

WHAT HAPPENED LATER?

Betty's family moved to Ontario in Canada. They built a new house and started a farm in a place called Waterloo. Betty's father bought land for his farm. He also bought some land to build a church on. All the families who moved to Waterloo with Betty's family came here for church.

Later on, Betty's brothers and sisters grew up and got married. Betty grew up too, but she did not get married. As she grew up, she could not learn things like other little girls. She had a difficult time doing things we do every day. She needed extra help with talking, math, and counting her numbers. She needed help with everything growing up. Betty's mommy and daddy helped her when she was little. And they kept helping her and caring for her after she grew up. Betty lived with her parents for the rest of her life.

Ah, Lord God! Behold, You have made the heavens and the earth by Your great power and outstretched arm. There is nothing too hard for You. (Jeremiah 32:17)

DISCUSSION QUESTIONS

1. What new country did Betty's family move to?
2. What did Betty ride in on the long trip?
3. Why was Betty scared?
4. What should we do when we are scared?
5. What does our Bible verse teach us?

Amicalola Falls State Park in Georgia

ELIAS BOUDINOT AND HIS PRINTING PRESS

17

Elias Boudinot was a Cherokee Indian. He was born in 1802. He lived with other Cherokees in Georgia in the United States of America. Elias was a printer. He used a printing press to make books and newspapers. He printed these in the Cherokee language. The Cherokees liked to read the books and newspapers Elias printed.

Each day, Elias went to a little house where his printing press was stored. He and other Cherokee men took little letters made of metal. They arranged them in lines. Each letter of the alphabet was its own little piece of metal. As Elias arranged the let-

Elias grew up in Georgia.

ters, he made words to read. Do you know what he was doing? He was getting ready to print a book. The letters he used were part of the big machine called a printing press.

What kinds of books do you think Elias printed? He printed books for children. These books helped children learn to read. They taught children each letter of the alphabet. Elias and his wife, Harriett, had six children. Elias and Harriett wanted all of their children to learn how to read.

What other books did Elias print? He printed books about farming, and he printed Bibles. These books helped people to learn about life. The Bibles taught people how to live well. And the farming books taught people how to farm well. Many of the Cherokee Indians were farmers.

Elias worked hard at his printing press. But he did not print the books all by himself. Other Cherokees helped him. An American missionary helped too. The missionary's name was Samuel Worcester. Samuel came to the Cherokee people to teach them about God. Samuel and Elias worked together at the printing press. Each week, they printed a newspaper for the Cherokee people to read. It was called the *Cherokee Phoenix*. The news-

A Cherokee barn. Cherokees used barns like this for their cows and other farm animals. They built their fences out of long pieces of wood.

paper told the important news that had happened that week. Elias also printed a chapter from the Bible in each newspaper. He put stories in the paper too. People liked to read the newspapers.

ELIAS HELPS SOMEONE IN TROUBLE

This is a page of Elias Boudinot's Cherokee newspaper. If you wrote a newspaper for your family, what important news would you put in it?

One day, Elias' friend Samuel got in trouble. Samuel tried to stop a man from stealing land from the Cherokees. The governor of Georgia became angry with Samuel. Soldiers came and arrested Samuel. They took him away to a prison in Georgia. They took

Samuel from his wife, Ann, and their two little daughters. Samuel's family cried and cried when the soldiers took Samuel away.

When Elias heard what had happened, he was sad too. He wanted to help his friend, but he could not get Samuel out of prison. What could he do? He prayed and asked God to set Samuel free. Then he helped take care of Samuel's wife and their little girls. He brought them food and other things they might need.

Elias Boudinot, the Cherokee Indian

But Elias wanted to help more. He knew Ann was upset because her husband, Samuel, was in prison. What could Elias do to help? He thought and thought. Then he came up with a plan. Elias went home and counted his money. He did not have much money, but he did have a little. He took some of the money and put it in his pocket. Then he went to see John Ross. John was a chief of the Cherokee Indians. Elias told Chief John his plan. John gave him some more money. Then Elias went to other Cherokee friends. They each gave him some money.

Finally, Elias thought he had enough money for his plan. He went to see Ann, the wife of Samuel. Elias took out all the money he had gathered and gave it to Ann.

"This is for you," he said. "Your husband Samuel is in prison, and we know you miss him. We want you to visit Samuel! But the prison is a long way from here, and the trip will cost a lot of money. Take this money and use it to pay for the trip. Use it to go visit your husband!

Ann was thrilled to see the money Elias had gathered. She was thrilled she would see her husband again!

"My wife and I will take care of your little girls too!" Elias said. "We will look after them while you are away." Ann was thankful. She knew her daughters would be well cared for while she was gone.

"Thank you, Elias!" Ann said.

Elias smiled. He was glad to give his money to Ann so she could see her husband, Samuel. "If you need more money, I will find it for you," he said. Elias remembered what the Bible says. It tells us, "Let no one seek his own good, but the good of his neighbor." (1 Corinthians 10:24 ESV). Elias wanted to help other people because he loved them.

Ann went to visit her husband, Samuel. Later on, the governor of Georgia let Samuel go free! He realized he was wrong to put Samuel in prison. Samuel's wife and children were happy to have him home. They were filled with joy to see Samuel again. All the Cherokee Indians were happy. They thanked God for bringing Samuel safely back to them.

WHAT HAPPENED LATER?

Later, many Cherokees were forced to find new homes. People came and took the land where the Indians lived. They told the Indians, "Move to a new place far, far away." Elias and his family left their home in Georgia to look for a new place to live.

Elias Boudinot took his family to a new home in Oklahoma. Samuel Worcester and his family moved to Oklahoma too. Elias and Samuel set up a new printing press in Oklahoma. They continued to print books and newspapers for the Cherokee people.

[Jesus said:] "This is My commandment, that you love one another as I have loved you." (John 15:12)

DISCUSSION QUESTIONS

1. What did Elias Boudinot make with his printing press?
2. What did Elias do when his friend Samuel was thrown into prison?
3. How could you help if one of your friends was in trouble?
4. What does our Bible verse teach us?

Blue Ridge Mountains, Virginia

CYRUS MCCORMICK AND HIS REAPER

Young Cyrus lay in bed, burning with a fever. For days, he had been ill, and his fever continued to grow worse and worse. Robert and Mary Ann were concerned for their son. "When will he get better?" they wondered. Robert called for the doctor. The doctor told Robert and Mary Ann, "Your son has yellow fever. I think we need to bleed him. It will help him recover."

At this time in history, doctors did not know as much as they do today. Many doctors thought that bleeding patients would help them heal. They would make a cut on the skin that caused the patient to bleed for hours. They thought that by making blood come out, they were forcing the disease out too. But this is not true! Later, scientists and doctors learned this was not a good way to heal sick people. In fact, it could make things worse, or even kill patients.

Cyrus' father was very wise. God gave him much wisdom and knowledge. He studied God's world carefully. Robert used the plants and herbs God created as tools to solve problems. Mr. McCormick did not believe bleeding would help his son. He told the doctor, "No, we do not want to bleed him. We will try something else." Robert gave his son hot baths, tea, and herbs. In time, Cyrus healed. He recovered completely from the dangerous yellow fever.

Little Cyrus was eager to get back to work! As soon as he was healthy again, he joined his family with the farm chores once again. There was always plenty of work to do on the McCormick farm. From the time the sun came up until long after the sun went down, there was work to do. The McCormick children liked to work hard on the farm.

Cyrus lived in Rockbridge County, Virginia, on a beautiful farm. Cyrus and his family lived off the land. They learned how to use every resource God created. The McCormick farm was like a construction factory. The McCormicks made their own shoes. They made their own clothes too. They used cotton, flax, and wool to weave beautiful patterns. If something grew on the land, it had a practical use.

On weekdays, Cyrus went to school. After finishing his morning chores, he would walk down the little dirt road with his books. Not far from the family farm, there was a one-room building made of logs. This was the schoolhouse. Cyrus studied five subjects at school. Math, Grammar, Spelling, the Bible, and the Westminster Shorter Catechism. As a little boy, Cyrus loved to study the Bible most of all. He knew that God's Word was the most important book to learn.

The McCormick farm in Rockbridge County, Virginia

Cyrus' favorite chapter in the Bible was Romans 8. This chapter in the Bible says:

What then shall we say to these things? If God is for us, who can be against us? For I am persuaded that . . . [nothing] shall be able to separate us from the love of God which is in Christ Jesus our Lord. (Romans 8:31, 38-39)

The McCormick farm included large wheat fields. The Lord blessed the land with rain and sunshine, causing the wheat to grow. But wheat will not harvest itself. It takes a lot of hard work and a lot of sweat to cut the wheat and collect it. Sowing seed into the ground is the first step. Have you ever planted seeds? It is fun to watch big plants grow from little seeds! But then, the plants must be reaped. Reaping means harvesting the big plants that have grown from the seeds. Harvesting wheat on the family farm was

Blacksmith shop (left) and grist mill (right) at the McCormick farm

When Cyrus McCormick was a boy, there were no big farm machines such as tractors like this one.

hard work. The days were hot and humid, and the sun shone strong and bright in the summer.

Today we have tractors and big machines to help us harvest wheat. But when Cyrus was a boy, every piece of wheat was harvested by hand. Can you guess what Cyrus and the farmworkers used to cut the wheat? They used sickles and scythes to cut the wheat. This is how people in the Bible cut wheat too! They used a special tool called a "grain cradle" to cut the stems and keep them together. Then they scooped the freshly cut grain into their arms. The golden wheat smelled sweet and good. Later, the bread would taste good too.

A farmer with a scythe

The grain cradle was easier to use than a scythe. But in the hot sun, on long days, it was still back-breaking work. By the end of the workday, Cyrus' back ached and his head hurt. Cyrus thought, "There must be a faster way to harvest all this wheat!"

Robert McCormick had the same idea. When Cyrus was seven, his father created something wonderful. He created a machine that could be pulled by two horses to cut down wheat. He called it a "reaper." But the first reaper did not work well. The grain became jammed in the reaper and the reaper would not cut. Robert was disappointed, but he kept working on his design for the reaper.

As Cyrus grew up, he began to work on his father's reaper idea. The challenge was exciting! He wanted his father's idea to work. Cyrus took his father's designs and figured out how to make them better. This is a good example of honoring your father's work and making it even better.

In 1831, when Cyrus was in his early twenties, he constructed a reaper that worked. The new reaper would not jam as easily. He took his reaper with two horses to a nearby village called Steel's Tavern. He staged a display. He wanted others to see the reaper at work. With the two horses and the reaper, Cyrus cut six acres of oats in one afternoon. It would have taken six farmworkers with scythes to do the same amount of work in that timeframe.

The reaper brought joy into the harvesting season. Farmers had more time to do other important things for God. Cyrus had done a very good thing! He had taken his father's idea and made a useful invention. The reaper would help people all over the world.

But Cyrus had to wait many years before his reaper became successful. Meanwhile, he worked on the reaper. He made it better and better. He sold it to other farmers. He waited for farmers to see how useful the reaper was. Finally, Cyrus' hard work paid off. He never gave up, and God saw this and blessed him. The Lord sent Cyrus buyers for his reaper. He sold seven reapers in 1842, twenty-nine reapers in 1843, and fifty reapers in 1844!

Over time, farmers throughout the world started using reapers. Within a few decades, almost every farm had one. The reaper made harvesting much easier. This gave more time to farmers and more food to everyone. This lowered food prices too. Farmers would say, "My reaper paid for itself in just one harvest!" In 1858, Senator Johnson of Maryland made a guess about the reaper's value. He said, "I think the

Cyrus McCormick's reaper at work

reaper has saved America $55 million in labor, this year alone!" That is a large number! We add value to the world by using our skills like Cyrus did. We bring glory to God by helping others.

WHAT HAPPENED LATER

Cyrus spent the rest of his life improving the reaper. He wanted his invention to be perfect. He sold it to as many farmers as he could. He was an honest and wise businessman. He wanted farmers to have confidence in the machine, so he made a promise. He said that it would pay for itself within a certain amount of time. If it did not, farmers could return the reaper and get all their money back from him.

Later, Cyrus moved to the city of Chicago. Chicago was the perfect city to sell a new machine. The city was a busy place in the 1860s and 1870s. And it was getting bigger by the day. Cyrus built a factory to make and sell his reapers. Soon, he could send them to farms from Virginia to California.

Cyrus knew the blessings of hard work. Through hard work, we glorify God, and we share the fruit of our labors with others. Because Cyrus worked so hard to create a reaper that worked well, others were blessed. The reaper gave people more time and saved them lots of money.

Cyrus also knew that we need God to bless our work if we will succeed. As the Bible says in Psalm 127:1, "Unless the LORD builds the house, those who build it labor in vain." Like Cyrus, we should work hard. And we should ask God to help us in our work to do a good job. We should also pray that God would use our work to bless others.

Cyrus Hall McCormick

Do you see a man who excels in his work?
He will stand before kings;
He will not stand before unknown men. (Proverbs 22:29)

DISCUSSION QUESTIONS

1. In what state of America did Cyrus grow up in?
2. What was Cyrus' favorite chapter of the Bible?
3. In what year did Cyrus build a reaper that worked?
4. What does our Bible verse teach us?

Louis Pasteur in his laboratory

LOUIS PASTEUR: A SCIENTIST HELPS A SICK LITTLE BOY

19

Louis Pasteur walked back and forth across the room. He was thinking hard. Mr. Pasteur was a scientist in France. For many years, he had studied germs. Do you know what a germ is? A germ is too tiny for you to see, but bad germs can make people incredibly sick.

Have you ever been sick? Have you ever had a cold or the flu? If you have, then germs were inside you. The germs were fighting the good things in your body. Your body fought off the bad germs, and you got better. But sometimes people stay sick for a long time from germs. They can even die if they have too many bad germs inside them.

Mr. Pasteur did not want people to get sick. He wanted to find a way to stop germs from hurting people. He knew that God created everything, even germs. And he knew God made special ways for us to fight germs. Mr. Pasteur said to himself, "Germs are so tiny that I can't see them. But if I can find out where germs live and how to kill them, then I can help sick people get better. And maybe I can help people to not get sick anymore." This was a good idea, but how could Mr. Pasteur find out these things?

Mr. Pasteur started studying germs. He studied all day long. He had a special building where he studied. The building was called a laboratory. Inside his laboratory, Mr. Pasteur used a microscope to look at germs. A microscope is a tool you can look into. It makes tiny things look big so we can see them.

Mr. Pasteur could see tiny things with his microscope. He could see things that nobody could see with their eyes. He could even see the littlest of germs. "These germs are so small," he thought. "How can I fight them?"

Mr. Pasteur began making medicine to fight the germs. He made special cages in his lab. Then he bought some chickens and some rabbits. Did you know that chickens and rabbits get sick just like people do? Mr. Pasteur gave the chickens and rabbits some of the medicine he made. The animals became healthy in no time at all. Mr. Pasteur's medicine was working!

Mr. Pasteur also bought some little white mice. He used these mice in his work on germs. He learned many things as he spent days and days studying and working with his animals.

This girl is looking into a microscope so she can see very tiny things.

A LITTLE BOY GETS SICK

Not far from Mr. Pasteur's home was a village called Steige. A little boy lived there. He was nine years old, and his name was Joseph Meister. One day in 1885, Joseph was walking by himself on a street. Suddenly, a dog ran up to him and bit him on the leg. The dog had a sickness called rabies. Joseph tried to run away, but the dog ran faster than he could. Joseph was scared, but some men came and helped him by chasing the dog away.

When Joseph's mother heard what had happened, she said, "We need help." She knew that rabies germs are deadly. They can spread like a fire and make us ill. Joseph's mother knew that bad germs went into Joseph when the sick dog bit him. Joseph might die if he did not have help. Joseph's mother said, "I will bring my son to Mr. Pasteur. He can help my son and stop this sickness."

Mr. Pasteur was still working in his laboratory. He was surprised to see Joseph and his mother.

"Please help us, Mr. Pasteur," Joseph's mother said. "Can you kill the germs before my son gets sick and dies?"

Mr. Pasteur looked at the bites on Joseph's legs. "The dog bit you hard, didn't he?" Mr. Pasteur asked. Joseph nodded. Joseph wondered what Mr. Pasteur would do. Then Mr. Pasteur smiled. "I think I can help," he said. "I think we can stop this sickness, and you will get better. You won't get sick and die."

Mr. Pasteur was happy to help. He made a special medicine for Joseph. He gave Joseph the medicine every day. And he let Joseph play with his animals. Joseph liked holding the chickens and rabbits. He enjoyed playing with the little white mice that Mr. Pasteur kept in his laboratory. Would you like to play with chickens and rabbits and mice?

Joseph Meister in 1885

Each day, Mr. Pasteur gave Joseph some medicine. It took a long time for all the medicine to work. While Joseph played and while he slept, the medicine was working inside him. It was fighting the bad germs from the dog bites. Can you guess what the medicine did? It killed all the germs, and Joseph got better.

Mr. Pasteur was incredibly happy that his medicine helped Joseph. After Joseph and his mother went home, Mr. Pasteur wrote letters to Joseph. He even sent presents to the little boy. When Joseph became a man, he decided to work at Mr. Pasteur's laboratory. Would you like to work there?

Louis Pasteur

WHAT HAPPENED LATER?

Mr. Pasteur spent the rest of his life studying germs. He studied many diseases that make people sick. He wanted to help people everywhere. People came from all over the world to see Mr. Pasteur and to learn how to make medicine. Mr. Pasteur worked hard to make special medicine. Now, people all over the world use this medicine to fight germs and stop sickness.

The LORD will give what is good.
(Psalm 85:12)

DISCUSSION QUESTIONS

1. When Mr. Pasteur wanted to learn about germs, what did he do?
2. What happened to the little boy who came to Mr. Pasteur for help?
3. Even if you aren't a scientist like Louis Pasteur, how can you help people who are sick?
4. Mr. Pasteur was glad God gave us things to fight sickness. What does our Bible verse teach us about God?

CHARLES SPURGEON AND HIS GRANDFATHER

Long ago, in 1834, a little boy was born in England. His name was Charles Spurgeon. He lived with his father and mother and brothers and sisters. Sometimes, Charles visited his grandparents.

Charles loved to go to his Grandfather Spurgeon's house. Grandfather lived in the country. Around his house the grass grew, and the birds sang in the trees. Inside the house were shelves full of books. Charles did not know how to read yet, but he loved to look at the books. He wondered what was inside them. Someday he would be able to read them too.

Grandfather Spurgeon was a pastor. He preached in a little church near his home. On Sunday mornings, Charles got dressed for church. His grandmother helped him put on his best clothes. Then she gave him a book with pictures in it and told him, "Sit quietly. Grandfather is working on his sermon."

Charles took his book and sat in the parlor. His grandfather was sitting at his desk with his Bible open. Charles looked at the pictures in his book. When he got tired of that, he looked around the room. He swung his legs back and forth as he sat in his chair. Was it time for church yet?

Grandfather looked up from his Bible. "Be quiet, my lad," he said.

Charles stopped swinging his legs and looked down at his book again. "I have to be quiet!" he told himself. "If I'm noisy, I'll distract Grandfather, and he won't finish his sermon. Then, people won't learn the way to heaven. How terrible!" Charles wanted people to love Jesus just like his grandfather did. He sat quietly and looked at his book until it was time to go to church.

Charles liked to look at his grandfather's books.

DON'T BE LATE FOR CHURCH!

As Charles grew older, he loved to tell people about Jesus. He loved Jesus, and he wanted other people to love Him too. Charles began preaching when he was a young man. God blessed him, and he became a great preacher.

One day, someone asked Charles to preach at their church. Charles was excited to preach, but the church was far away. He could not walk to the church, so he rode on a train to get there.

The train traveled very quickly. Charles knew he would get to the church in time. But suddenly, the train started to slow down. "What happened?" Charles asked. Something was wrong with the train. A repairman began to fix it. Charles waited and waited. Would he get to the church in time after all? The repairman worked and worked. Finally, the train was fixed. It started moving again. "What will happen if I don't get to church in time to preach?" Charles wondered.

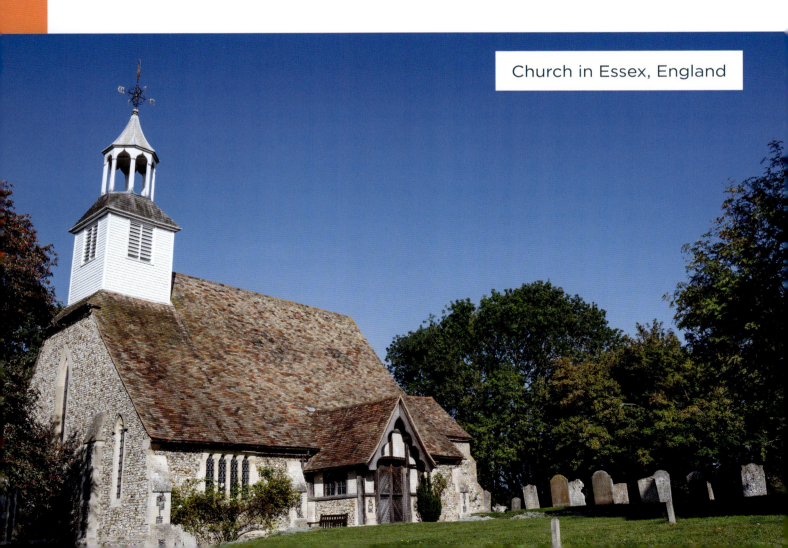

Church in Essex, England

When Charles arrived at the church, the service had already started. The people had sung hymns to worship God. Then it had been time to preach. Charles could hear someone preaching as he ran up to the church. He was too late! Can you guess what happened?

Charles slipped quietly into the back of the church. He looked up at the pulpit. Who was preaching? Do you know who it was?

It was Charles' grandfather! Since Charles was late, the people had asked his grandfather to preach instead. Grandfather Spurgeon was preaching about God's grace. "We are bad people," he said. "We do bad things. The bad things we do are called sin. But God loves to save people who sin. He saves us even though we are bad and don't deserve to be saved. This is called grace, God's grace."

As Grandfather Spurgeon preached, he saw Charles walk into the church. Grandfather pointed at Charles. "Here comes my grandson!" he said. Charles walked down the aisle. Grandfather Spurgeon moved aside so Charles could finish the sermon.

Charles walked up to the pulpit. His grandfather told him, "I was preaching on

God's grace." Charles smiled. "I can finish that sermon," he said. He knew exactly what his grandfather would tell the people about God's grace. Charles began preaching to the church. Sometimes, his grandfather would come and stand beside him. He would tell the people something he wanted to say. Together, Grandfather Spurgeon and Charles finished the sermon.

WHAT HAPPENED LATER?

As Charles grew older, he kept preaching. He was a good preacher. People called him "the Prince of Preachers." For the rest of his life, Charles told people about Jesus. Sometimes, he would think about all the things his grandfather had taught him. When he thought about these things, he smiled. "Grandfather told people about God. Now I am telling people about God," he thought. "God loves His people so much that He sends men to teach them. I am so happy that Jesus lets me tell people about Him!"

For by grace you have been saved through faith, and that not of yourselves; it is the gift of God. (Ephesians 2:8)

DISCUSSION QUESTIONS

1. Why did Charles have to keep quiet while his grandfather studied?
2. What made Charles late for the church service?
3. Why did Charles love to tell other people about Jesus?
4. What does our Bible verse teach us?

This is a picture of the inside of the Metropolitan Tabernacle Church in London, England. This is where Charles Spurgeon preached God's Word for many years.

Japan is a land filled with flowers.
This picture is near Tokyo, where Neesima was born.

JOSEPH NEESIMA: A SOLDIER OR A TEACHER? 21

Have you ever been to Japan? It is a group of islands in the Pacific Ocean near China. It is a land filled with beautiful flowers. Today, Japan has cars and radios and airplanes. But long ago, it did not have these things. Almost two hundred years ago, in 1843, a little boy was born in Japan. His name was Neesima.

Would you like to ride in a jinrikisha? Would you like to pull one?

Neesima was born in Tokyo, the capital city of Japan. When Neesima was a little boy, Tokyo did not have cars or trains. If people wanted to travel somewhere in the city, they had to walk. Or they could use a jinrikisha. Do you know what a jinrikisha is? It is a little carriage or cart that is pulled by a person instead of a horse.

When Neesima ate food, he did not use a fork or a spoon like we do. In Japan, everyone used chopsticks to eat with. Even little girls and boys used chopsticks.

Neesima liked to eat with chopsticks. He also liked to look at all the pretty flowers growing in Tokyo. There were many trees in Tokyo that had pink blossoms. They were called cherry trees. Neesima knew that cherry trees started out as tiny seeds. Then, they grew into small plants. Then, they grew bigger and

Boys and girls in Japan learned to eat their food with chopsticks.

bigger. When a little cherry tree was planted in a tiny pot, it would grow so big it would break the pot. Then it would grow bigger and bigger until it was big enough for Neesima to climb the tree and play in its branches.

Neesima's father was a samurai. Do you know what that is? A samurai is a warrior or soldier who carries a special sword wherever he goes. Neesima wanted to grow up to be just like his father. He dreamed about the day when he would be old enough to have a special sword just like his father. Then he would be a man too.

But one day Neesima thought, "Maybe I shouldn't be a soldier." He looked around at all the beautiful trees and flowers growing in Tokyo. "God made all the trees and all the flowers," he thought to himself. "And God made all the people too. Maybe I should be a teacher instead of a soldier. I could help people learn more about God."

Neesima began studying. He studied for many years. He wanted to learn many things so he could teach other people. When he got older, he even traveled on a boat all the way to the United States of America to learn things. Then he sold his special samurai sword. Neesima sold his sword and bought a Bible.

Neesima learned many things in America. Then he went back to Japan. He bought a piece of land and built a school for children. Then he began teaching them all the things he had learned.

Neesima said: "There are many children in Japan, and I can only teach a few of them. But God can use these boys and girls that I teach, and they can teach other people. We are like the little cherry tree. We are a little seed planted in a tiny pot. But soon the little seed will grow into a little plant. Then it will break out of the pot. It will grow so big that no one can stop it from growing!"

Cherry trees start out small, but if you leave them in a little pot, they will grow so big that they will break the pot. Then they will grow into a big tree.

Then He [Jesus] said, "What is the kingdom of God like? And to what shall I compare it? It is like a mustard seed, which a man took and put in his garden; and it grew and became a large tree, and the birds of the air nested in its branches." (Luke 13:18-19)

DISCUSSION QUESTIONS

1. What country was Neesima from?
2. How did people in Japan travel without any cars or horses?
3. Why did Neesima go to America?
4. What did Neesima do when he came back to Japan?
5. What does our Bible verse teach us?

Mele Maat Cascades in Port Vila, Efate Island, Vanuatu

KAHI GETS MARRIED

22

Kahi was a little girl born around 1851. She lived on an island in a place called Vanuatu. Vanuatu is a group of islands. They are in the South Pacific Ocean near Australia. Do you see them on the map?

Kahi's island was called Aniwa (Uh-NEE-wah). She lived in a small village with her family. Many other families lived in her village too. Kahi's home was a little hut with tree branches for a roof. Her little island was full of trees. Coconut trees rose high above her. Kahi liked the coconut trees. Their feathery branches waved in the wind,

and when the coconuts were ripe, her father would cut them open. Kahi and her siblings would watch eagerly as the top of the thick, yellow-green husk was whacked off. Then, they would drink the sweet milk and eat the white meat hidden deep inside.

    Beside the village was the ocean. Kahi liked to play in the waves as they crashed against the shore. The ocean was important for the people who lived on Aniwa. The men fished in the ocean. They brought home flying fish for the women to cook. The ocean also helped the people stay clean. Kahi's home did not have a bathtub in it. Whenever Kahi got dirty, she went to the beach to get clean. She took baths in the salty ocean water.

    Not far from Kahi's house was the church. The men of the village had helped to build the church. Their pastor was a missionary, John Paton. Mr. Paton showed the men how to build the church. They cut down tall trees. Then the men formed a line and carried a tree on their shoulders. It was hard work.

    Kahi could not help with the trees, but she could help in another way. The women

The roof of this house in Vanuatu is made of branches.

The church on Aniwa

of the village needed branches from the coconut trees. Kahi and the other children helped carry the branches. The mothers braided the branches to make a roof for the church. The coconut-branch roof kept the rain away. It kept the people in the church safe and dry.

Mr. Paton had a wife named Maggie. Kahi liked Mrs. Paton. She taught the girls how to sew clothes and how to make hats. She also taught them new songs to sing. Kahi loved to hear the singing, and she liked to sing the songs about Jesus. She learned many things from Mrs. Paton. Mr. and Mrs. Paton had come all the way from Scotland. They had come to teach the people of Aniwa about Jesus.

KAHi GETS MARRiED

Kahi worked very hard learning to sew. She spent a lot of time with Mrs. Paton. The people on her island learned to love Mr. and Mrs. Paton. They learned to love

God too. When Kahi woke up in the mornings, she could hear people singing songs, praising God.

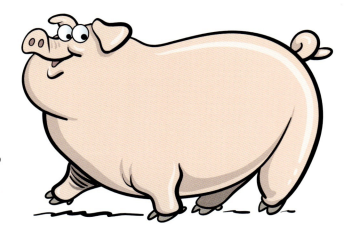

When Kahi grew older, it was time for her to get married. A man named Ropu loved her and wanted to marry her. When a man got married on Aniwa, he gave gifts to the bride's family. Can you guess what presents Ropu gave to Kahi's family? He gave them a few fat pigs. Kahi's family thought this was a wonderful gift. Do you think you would like fat pigs for a present?

Soon it was time for the wedding. The people on the island decorated the new church building. Kahi was nervous, but Mrs. Paton helped her get ready for the spe-

Vanuatu Beach

cial day. She helped Kahi sew special new clothes to wear, and she found a beautiful hat for her to put on. Then she gave her a bright red handkerchief to hold. Kahi smiled when she saw the handkerchief; it was very pretty!

When Kahi was all dressed, she hurried to the church. All the people were inside waiting. Mr. Paton was standing at the front of the church waiting too. Ropu smiled when he saw how beautiful Kahi was in her special new clothes. He was glad to have a wife, and Kahi was glad to get married.

Now she and Ropu could start their own family. One day, Kahi would have little children of her own. Then, she would hold them and sing to them. She would teach them how to drink milk from a coconut. Kahi and Ropu would bring their children to church to hear Mr. Paton teach them about God. Then, on Sunday evenings, all the people of Aniwa would gather under a large banyan tree. They would pray together and sing songs as the sun set and the stars shone in the sky.

It was quiet all over the island. The ocean waves crashed against the beach, and the coconut branches waved in the wind. Kahi and the village people sat still under the banyan tree and sang praises to God. Maybe this was the part of the day that Kahi liked most of all.

Coconut fruit

Sing to the Lord a new song,
And His praise from the ends of the earth,
You who go down to the sea, and all that is in it,
You coastlands and you inhabitants of them!
(Isaiah 42:10)

DISCUSSION QUESTIONS

1. What kind of trees grew on Kahi's island?
2. What did Kahi do when she got dirty?
3. What did the people on Aniwa do on Sundays?
4. What does our Bible verse teach us?

Jungle forests of Vanuatu

Grist mill in Missouri

GEORGE WASHINGTON CARVER FINDS A SPECIAL GIFT FROM GOD 23

Long ago, around 1864, a little boy was born by the name of George. He was born in Missouri in the United States. George's daddy died before he was born, and George's mommy was missing. She went missing after George was born. George became the child of Moses and Susan Carver. Mr. and Mrs. Carver named George "George Carver" and took care of him.

When George was a little boy, he loved to wander in the woods. He loved to find pretty plants and flowers to bring home. He would carefully dig these up and carry them back home. Then he would plant them in a little garden he started beside his house. George loved to watch his plants and flowers

The home of Moses Carver, where George grew up

grow. Soon, he learned so much about plants that people came to see him. They asked him questions about plants even though he was a little boy.

When George Carver grew up, he kept studying plants.

"Why do you study plants so much?" people asked him.

George answered: "In the Bible, God told Adam and Eve, 'I have given you every herb (or plant) and every tree whose fruit yields seed; to you it shall be for food.' These plants and trees are good gifts. God gave them to us because they are good for

Just like this little boy, George Carver loved to grow plants and flowers.

us. These plants can make us strong and healthy. They have special things inside them to help us stay well."

George Carver wanted to study plants and find the special things God had put inside each one. He started studying peanuts. Did you know that peanuts grow under the ground? Then, when they are ready for eating, people dig them up to eat them. George studied peanuts and learned how to make many things from them. He made peanut milk. Then, he made peanut oil. He made peanut ice cream and peanut paint and all kinds of things from peanuts.

When people heard about the things George Carver made from peanuts, they came to talk with him. They wanted to see everything he had made. People started to call him Dr. Carver. Some of the things Dr. Carver made were good to eat. Some things were good for sick people. George's peanut oil helped children whose arms or legs did not work.

George Washington Carver Finds a Special Gift from God

A LITTLE BOY WHO COULD NOT WALK

One day in 1934, a father brought his young son, Teddy, to see Dr. Carver. Teddy's father carried Teddy into Dr. Carver's room.

"What's wrong?" asked Dr. Carver.

"Teddy can't walk," his father said. Poor little Teddy was five years old. When he was a baby he had had a sickness that made his legs stop working. He could not stand or walk or run. All he could do was sit.

Dr. Carver looked at Teddy's legs. "Maybe I can help," he smiled. "Teddy, did you know that God gave us wonderful things in plants? Plants give us food, and they also help our bodies work well." Dr. Carver picked up a bottle of peanut oil. "This oil comes from peanuts," he explained to Teddy. "I'll rub it on your legs, and maybe it will help them get strong again."

Dr. Carver rubbed the peanut oil on Teddy's legs. "You need to use this oil every day," he told Teddy's father. "Bring Teddy back each week, and I will work on his legs until they are well."

Each week, Teddy's father or mother carried him into Dr. Carver's room. Dr. Carver gently rubbed Teddy's legs with peanut oil.

God made peanuts grow underground. When they are fully grown, we can dig them up and eat them.

"Will I be able to walk one day?" Teddy asked.

"Maybe you will," Dr. Carver said.

Days passed. Then weeks passed. Still, Teddy could not walk. But Dr. Carver kept working on his legs.

One month passed. Then two months passed. Then three months. Finally, a few days before Christmas, Teddy felt his legs getting stronger. His father took him to see Dr. Carver again. That day, when Dr. Carver finished rubbing his legs, Teddy did not wait for his father to pick him up. He stood up on his own and walked across the room. He did not need to be carried.

"I can walk!" Teddy said. "My legs are all better now!"

Dr. Carver smiled a big smile. He was glad Teddy was getting better. Dr. Carver said, "I want to help people as long as I live. I want them to see the beautiful, helpful things God made. Jesus loves me, and I want to love other people. I want to help people be strong and healthy. I am happy that God made me and this beautiful world. I am happy that I can help people see all the wonderful things He created."

George Washington Carver Finds a Special Gift from God

And God said, "See, I have given you every herb . . . and every tree." . . . Then God saw everything that He had made, and indeed it was very good....
(Genesis 1:29, 31)

DISCUSSION QUESTIONS

1. What did George Carver like to do when he was a little boy?
2. What are some things George made with peanuts?
3. How did Dr. Carver help Teddy get better?
4. What does our Bible verse teach us about the things God made?

George Washington Carver

Beach in Thailand

FA-YING OF SIAM: A PRINCESS AND A VERY SPECIAL PERSON

24

Fa-Ying was a princess. She was born in 1855. She lived in a beautiful palace with her father and all her family in a kingdom called Siam. (Today we call it Thailand.) Fa-Ying's father was King Mongkut. He was the king of Siam. He ruled over all the people in his kingdom.

Siam was a kingdom with lots of people and lots of animals. Thick, dark jungles filled parts of the kingdom. In these jungles lived many creatures. Elephants, tigers, rhinoceroses, and monkeys lived there. The king of Siam lived in his palace in a city called Bangkok. Sometimes, he traveled around his kingdom. He looked after all his people. And he looked after all the animals too. Whenever he traveled, he took Fa-Ying with him.

Siam (Thailand) is a country in the southern part of Asia.

Fa-Ying was a princess of Siam.

Princess Fa-Ying loved her father, and he loved her. Everywhere the king of Siam went, Fa-Ying went with him. Even when she was a little baby, her father carried her with him. He held her in his lap when he traveled in his royal carriage.

Fa-Ying loved to travel with her father. Every day was exciting. Near the palace was a large river called the Chao Phraya. Sometimes, the king traveled on the river. He had a royal boat that carried him up and down the river. Fa-Ying liked to ride on the boat. She liked to watch the water rush by as men rowed the boat. Would you like to ride in a royal boat with a king?

A BIG SURPRISE

One day, a special messenger came to the palace. "I have news for the king!" he said. He was excited.

Princess Fa-Ying was excited too. She wondered what the important news was. The messenger bowed in front of the king.

"We have found a white elephant in the jungle!" the messenger said.

This was very good news! The people of Siam loved elephants, but they liked white elephants best of all. They thought white elephants were very special.

The king smiled. "Bring the elephant here!" he commanded. "We will make it a special home beside the palace."

Elephants were very special to the people of Siam. Have you ever ridden on an elephant?

Workers began to build the special home at once. The workers built a special boat too. What do you think happened when the elephant came out of the jungle? The people led it to the special elephant boat! The boat was waiting on the river. The boat was big enough to hold the elephant. Red curtains decorated the sides of the boat, and the roof was covered with thousands of beautiful flowers. Fa-Ying and her father went to the river to meet the elephant. They brought sugarcane and special grass for the elephant to eat.

What do you think the white elephant thought of its boat? Do you think it liked to eat the sugarcane and grass that Fa-Ying brought it?

Soon it was time for Princess Fa-Ying to go back to the palace and get ready for bed. She was so happy to have a white elephant living near her that it was hard for her to fall asleep.

A NEW TEACHER

Every day, something new and exciting happened to Fa-Ying. When she

All the children in the palace were excited to see the white elephant.

was seven, someone special came to live at her house. The king invited a teacher to come live in the palace and teach his children. She would teach them how to speak English. The teacher's name was Anna Leonowens.

When Princess Fa-Ying saw Mrs. Anna, she was surprised. "That lady doesn't look like us," she said to herself. "And that lady doesn't dress like us either. Look at her big dresses! I wonder why she wears those instead of the clothes that we wear."

Mrs. Anna smiled when she met Fa-Ying. Fa-Ying smiled back. Soon, she became friends with Mrs. Anna. Fa-Ying liked to learn English because Mrs. Anna was a nice teacher. She let Fa-Ying climb up into her lap and listen as she told exciting stories.

What kind of stories do you think Mrs. Anna told? She told stories about long, long ago when God created the earth. She told Fa-Ying that God made all the trees and all the elephants and all the people. He made everything! Fa-Ying had never heard about this God before.

Mrs. Anna wore large dresses that the Siamese ladies and girls had never seen before.

"God made everything?" Fa-Ying asked in surprise.

"Yes, He did," said Mrs. Anna.

"Did He make the white elephant?" Fa-Ying asked.

Mrs. Anna smiled. "Yes, God even made the white elephant."

Then Mrs. Anna told a story about Jesus. Fa-Ying had never heard about Jesus before. She liked to listen to Mrs. Anna's stories. Soon, Fa-Ying began to love Jesus too. She knew her daddy was the king of Siam, but Jesus was the king of the whole world!

"God made all the people in Siam," Fa-Ying said. "And God made me! I'm very glad He made me." Fa-Ying smiled up into Mrs. Anna's face. "I love Jesus very much," she said.

Fa-Ying went to school each day and learned more and more from Mrs. Anna. Then, one day, something very sad happened. When Fa-Ying was eight years old, she became very sick.

Anna Leonowens

The king of Siam was worried. He called all his doctors and told them to help his little girl. The doctors tried to help, but Fa-Ying was too sick. Nobody could make her well again. Soon, little Fa-Ying died. Mrs. Anna was very sad to see Fa-Ying die, but she was glad that Jesus would take care of the little princess in heaven.

Jesus said, "Let the little children come to Me, and do not forbid them; for of such is the kingdom of heaven." (Matthew 19:14)

DISCUSSION QUESTIONS

1. Where did Princess Fa-Ying live?
2. How did the people of Siam bring the white elephant up the river to the palace?
3. What did Mrs. Anna teach Fa-Ying?
4. What does our Bible verse teach us?

Idanre Hills, Nigeria

MARY SLESSOR: THE RED-HAIRED LADY AND THE TWIN BABIES

25

Mary Slessor was born in 1848 in Scotland. She had six brothers and sisters. Mary was a short little girl with red hair. Do you think all her brothers and sisters had red hair too?

When Mary grew up, she left Scotland and moved to Africa in 1876. Mary went to a place called Nigeria. Do you see it on the map? Nigeria is full of jungles and wild animals.

The people who lived in Nigeria did very bad things. They liked to fight and kill each other. Mary wanted to help them. She wanted to teach the people of Nigeria about Jesus. She said, "I love Jesus, and I want these people to love Jesus too."

Mary Slessor

The people of Nigeria were surprised to see Mary with her red hair. All the people in Nigeria had black hair. They had never seen a red-haired person before.

Mary talked to the people and told them about God. She told them about the truth of Jesus. She told them that Jesus wanted to save them and give them new lives. But the people shook their heads. They did not believe the things Mary told them. They did not believe in Jesus.

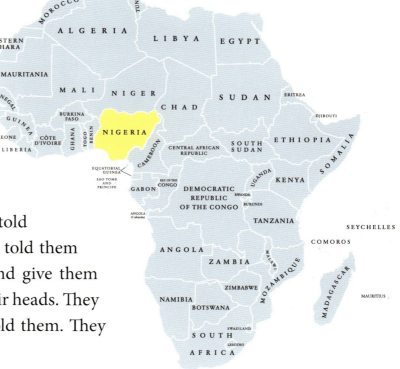

"You are a strange woman," they said. "You don't look like us, and you don't act like us. Why should we listen to you?" The people walked away and kept doing bad things.

Mary began praying for the people. She lived in a little hut in the jungle near the people she wanted to help. Every day she prayed that God would teach these people what was right and wrong. She prayed that God would teach these people to love Him. Mary was glad she could talk to Jesus about these people she loved. She knew He loved the people of Nigeria even more than she did. He wanted them to stop fighting each other and start loving God and one another.

When Mary came to Nigeria, the people there didn't trust her.

The people in Nigeria lived in huts instead of houses. Mary lived in a hut too.

One day, Mary heard a shout in the jungle. She ran out of her hut to see what had happened. Everyone in the village was very angry. Why were they angry? A woman had just had a baby. Do you think the people were happy to see the new baby? No, they were not happy. They were not happy because the woman had two babies. She had twins. Do you know what twins are? Twins are two babies who are born at the same time.

The people in the village shouted angrily. "It isn't right for a woman to have two babies at the same time!" they said. "We must kill the babies!"

Mary ran up to the people and tried to stop them. "You mustn't kill the babies!" she said. "It isn't right to kill babies. We must love them and care for them."

But the people would not listen. So Mary's heart filled with love for the babies. She took the little children and brought them to her home. "I'll protect these babies," she said. "I won't let anyone hurt them."

The babies were hungry, so Mary bought milk and fed them. Then she wrapped them up in blankets and rocked them to sleep.

When the people in Nigeria saw what Mary Slessor had done, they shook their

heads. "Why did she do that?" they asked. "The babies will die. And she will waste all her money giving them milk to drink and taking care of them."

But Mary knew she was not wasting her money. She knew it was right to take care of the babies. She loved them even though no one else did.

It was not long before another mother had twin babies. The people tried to kill these babies too, so the mother gave them to Mary.

"Will you take care of these babies?" she asked.

Asoquo was a cute baby, but he could get into trouble.

Mary Slessor: The Red-Haired Lady and the Twin Babies

"I know you will love my babies. You won't let them die."

"Yes," said Mary. She took the babies and brought them to her hut. "My family is getting bigger and bigger!" Mary laughed. Soon she had babies filling her home. It was hard work to take care of them all. Mary fed the babies and dressed them and took care of them. She named one of the girls Jean. When Jean grew up to be as old as you are, she could help Mary with the other children. Mary was glad for the help. Sometimes she had nine babies all staying in her house at the same time!

Mary Slessor and some of her children. Jean is the child at left.

Mary Slessor and her family

One of the babies was a little boy named Asoquo. He had big eyes and a big smile. But Asoquo was very naughty. He was always getting into trouble. When nobody was looking, he would crawl away and eat the food in the cat's bowl. Mary had to keep an eye on him!

The people of Nigeria watched as Mary took care of all those little babies. "Why do you love them?" they asked. "Why do you work so hard to take care of them?"

"I love them just like I love all of you," Mary explained. "I came all the way from Scotland to love you people of Nigeria. I want you to understand what is good and what is right. I want you to learn about Jesus and love Him just like I do."

The people of Nigeria nodded. "Now we understand," they said. "Mary Slessor doesn't look like us. She has red hair, and our hair is black. She doesn't act like us either. But she loves us."

The people came and sat inside Mary's hut, and she began to teach them about God. Mary was very happy. The people of Nigeria were happy too. They learned to love God, and they loved Mary very much too. They called her the mother of all the people of Nigeria.

Beloved, let us love one another, for love is of God; and everyone who loves is born of God and knows God. (1 John 4:7)

DISCUSSION QUESTIONS

1. Mary Slessor was born in Scotland. What country did she move to in Africa?
2. What did the people of Nigeria think when they saw Mary for the first time?
3. What did Mary do with the twin babies that nobody wanted?
4. How did the people learn to love God?
5. What does our Bible verse teach us?

CHI WANG: MOTHER IN THE FAITH TO THE SEDIQ CHRISTIANS

26

Up in the mountains of Taiwan, there lived a group of people known as the Sediq tribe. In 1895, life became difficult for the Sediq tribe. That was the year the Japanese took control of the island.

Now, the Japanese ruled the island of Taiwan. They were often unkind to the people of Taiwan who had come from China. They were cruel to the native tribes, like the Sediq people. The Sediq people did not want to be ruled by Japan. They fought with the Japanese. The Japanese said, "We will set fire to the hills and destroy the Sediq."

But before that could happen, a woman named Chi Wang helped stop the fighting. Can you guess what she did? She helped the Japanese and Sediq to make peace. Chi Wang was from the Sediq people. But Chi Wang could speak both the Japanese and Taiwanese languages. Since Chi Wang could speak both languages, she could help the Japanese and Sediq be at peace with each other. Speaking more than one language can be a great gift to others!

Chi Wang convinced her people that it would be best to surrender to the Japanese. If they did not, they would be destroyed. The Japanese listened to Chi Wang, and they gave her gifts. They treated her well because she brought peace.

Now, there was peace between the Japanese and Sediq people. This was a good thing. But even though the Sediq had peace with the Japanese, they still did not know about the real God. They did not know about the greatest Peace Giver of all. They did not know that they could be saved from their sins.

Japanese soldiers entering Taipei, Taiwan

Christians had been living on Taiwan since the 1600s. But the Sediq people had not heard about Jesus Christ. They had not heard the good news that Jesus had come to save them. They did not know about the most important thing in life. Like many other tribes, they worshiped the creation, not God.

Who would bring them the good news about Jesus? How would the Sediq people be saved from their sins? Someone needed to tell them about the Savior, Jesus, who had come to help them.

God had more plans for Chi Wang. She had already brought peace between the Japanese and the Sediq tribe. But the Sediq needed more than peace with the Japanese. They needed peace with God. And Chi Wang needed peace with God too.

One day, in 1924, a preacher named Mr. Waterwheel Lee met Chi Wang. Pastor Lee was a shepherd of God's people in the village of Hualien.

Pastor Lee heard a woman sobbing in a back room of the house. He went to see who it was. Who did he find? He found Chi Wang crying and crying. She was very sad. "Why should I keep living?" she moaned. "I feel like my life is a waste." Then Pastor Lee comforted her. He shared the good news about Jesus with her. He told her that Jesus came to bring hope to hopeless people like her. "Chi Wang, all your sins will be forgiven if you trust Jesus," he said. Chi Wang rejoiced to hear the good news. She began attending church. She began reading the Bible too.

When Chi Wang was fifty-two years old, she was baptized. Chi Wang was so happy to be a new creation in Christ. She told everyone about the great joy Jesus had given her.

But as a Sediq woman, the Taiwanese and Japanese both treated her poorly. The people of Taiwan thought the Sediq people were savages. They thought the Sediq people did not know how to think or how to act. Chi Wang told the people of Taiwan, "You call me savage. But it is you who are acting like savages. I have accepted Christ, and you have refused Him."

Chi Wang was living among the Taiwanese. But she wanted her own people, the Sediq, to know the joy of being saved by Jesus.

Do you think it was easy for Chi Wang to share about Jesus with her people? No, it was not. The Japanese who ruled Taiwan said, "You must not talk about religion." They made a rule that no religion could be shared with the native tribes. The Sediq were a native tribe, so they could not hear about Jesus. "We want Shintoism to

Coast of Taiwan

become the faith of all the tribes," the Japanese said. "It is strictly forbidden to teach about the Christian faith."

But Chi Wang would share about Jesus anyway. She would risk her life to share the good news with her people. Besides, she was a native Sediq. She knew how to speak their language.

Before she did this, she attended a Bible school for two years. The school was called The Women's Missionary Society. The Presbyterian Church sent Chi Wang to the Sediq. How did Chi Wang share about Jesus? She began meeting with the men of the tribe. She told them what she was learning in the Bible.

The Missionary Society loved the Sediq tribe. They knew the tribe was hungry too. So the Society sent rice with Chi Wang. The rice would fill their stomachs, and the Bible would fill their souls. This is how Chi Wang showed love to her people. She brought them all the things they needed the most. As Chi Wang began to share about Jesus, more and more Sediq people listened. They wanted to follow Jesus. They wanted Him to be their Lord and Savior. At last, the church of Jesus was established among the Sediq people.

In the 1940s, a war began around the world. We call this war World War II. Japan still controlled Taiwan when the war began. Life became very difficult for the Christians of Taiwan when Japan went to war with America. Japan thought all Christians supported America—even the Christians in Taiwan. They thought this way because so many Americans were Christians.

Christians living in Taiwan began to suffer. They were beaten and put in prison. Sediq Christians were treated this way too, but they kept on meeting. Can you guess where they met? They worshiped the Lord on the sides of mountains, hidden by trees and rocks. They met in caves. They posted guards near the edge of their worship meetings. Do you think this was exciting or scary? If the Japanese came, the Sediq Christians would run and hide.

During the dark days of the war, Chi Wang kept teaching the Sediq people. She encouraged young men to study God's Word. She encouraged them to learn about God and their new faith in Him. She said, "After you learn what the Bible teaches, you can go teach others! You can tell other people about how Jesus saves sinners."

Chi Wang and a Sediq Christian

Chi Wang told one young man, "Do not start preaching for three months. Make sure you understand what you believe. Then, go and tell others about Jesus!"

A missionary asked the young man, "Did you follow what she said?"

"No!" he answered with joy. "I could hardly wait a week! Before I had completed my studies, I had won 25 people to Christ!"

Soon, more and more of the Sediq people began to follow Jesus. They heard about God and wanted to share about Him with others. One by one, the Sediq people were saved from their sins by Jesus.

Chi Wang also taught the new Christians that they should grow in their faith and knowledge. She said, "You must study your Bibles! Never stop praying."

Chi Wang: Mother in the Faith to the Sediq Christians

The war ended in 1945. Only one year later, Chi Wang finished her work on earth. She died and went to be with her Lord Jesus who loved her so much. She was seventy-four years old when she died. She had finished the race of faith. God had used her to bring the good news of Jesus the Messiah to her people. The Sediq Christians were thankful that God had sent Chi Wang. Like a mother in the faith, she had brought them the truth.

Chi Wang Memorial Church

Later, in 1961, a church was built called the "Chi Wang Memorial Church." It was built near a cave where the Sediq Christians once met for worship. By 1962, there were around 70,000 Christians living on the island of Taiwan. Many of them were Sediq. The good news that Jesus reigns and saves had come to the peoples of Taiwan. Praise be to God!

The Lord reigns;
Let the earth rejoice;
Let the multitude of isles be glad! (Psalm 97:1)

DISCUSSION QUESTIONS

1. What nation ruled Taiwan when Chi Wang became a Christian?
2. What was the name of Chi Wang's native people?
3. How old was Chi Wang when she became a Christian and was baptized?
4. Why does the Bible verse say the islands should rejoice?

Alec grew up in Ayrshire, Scotland.

ALEXANDER FLEMING RESCUES THE SHEEP

27

Alec Fleming was a little boy who lived with his family on a farm in Scotland. Scotland is a land filled with mountains, hills, and beautiful green fields. Do you see it on the map?

In 1886, Alec was five years old. His real name was Alexander Fleming, but everyone called him Alec. He lived with his family in a little farmhouse surrounded

by wide fields, rolling hills, and running streams. Every morning, Alec would walk through the fields with his father and brothers. He would help bring in the cows for milking. His family drank the milk. His mother used the milk to make delicious cheese to eat.

Alec's father owned hundreds of sheep, too. The sheep wandered all over the fields, eating grass and playing in the sunshine. Alec liked to help take care of the sheep. Have you ever held a baby sheep? It is soft and woolly and loves to play. Alec helped take care of the lambs.

Beautiful green grass filled the fields around Alec's house. But when winter came, blizzards came and the green fields filled with snow. Do you know what a blizzard is? Blizzards are strong snow storms. Scotland has many blizzards in the winter.

Alec knew when a blizzard was coming. He could hear the wind begin to howl. The clouds would become thick and dark, and the sun would disappear. The wind would swirl down from the mountains. Around the house it would swirl. The wind would bring cold, cold air to the farm. The wind would be so strong it could blow Alec off his feet. Then, the snow would come. During a blizzard, snow would fall and cover everything. It would cover the fields, the hills, and even Alec's house.

One day, an especially strong storm blew down from the mountains. Alec and his family stayed inside when the blizzard came. They lit a warm fire in the fireplace. They waited for the storm to stop. Outside the window, Alec watched as the snow piled higher and

A baby sheep is called a lamb.

When a blizzard comes, sheep don't know how to keep safe.

higher. Soon it covered the windows and doors and Alec could not see outside anymore. All he could see was white.

As soon as the storm ended, it was time to get to work.

"We must find the sheep before they die," Alec's father told him. "Come along, laddie. You can help."

Alec and his brothers put on their thick coats and boots to go outside with their father. When Alec stepped outside, he stopped and looked around. The world was white. Nothing could be seen except miles and miles of white. Alec knew they had to find the flock of sheep before all the sheep died in the snow.

Where do you think sheep go during a blizzard? When the winds begin to howl and the snow begins to fall, sheep get nice and cozy. They huddle together to stay warm. They look for a low spot in the fields, where the wind cannot reach them. Sheep think they will be safe here, but they are not safe. Sheep are not smart! The low spot keeps them safe from wind, but not snow. Sheep do not know how to climb out of snow, so they stand still and wait. They wait while the snow piles higher and higher on top of them.

Soon all the sheep in Alec's family's field were covered in snow. But the snow did not stop. It kept falling and falling. By the time the blizzard was over, the sheep were buried deep, deep down under the snow.

Alec and his family trudged through the snow-covered fields. They had to find the sheep before they died. But how could they find them buried under all that snow? Everything was covered in snow, and no one knew where the sheep had gone in the storm. How could they find out where the flock was buried?

"Look for a blowhole," Alec's father said.

Alec knew what his father meant. God made snow in a special way. Sheep keep breathing even when they are buried under snow. Their breath is warm. It melts a little of the cold snow that covers them. Soon a little hole can open up over the top of them. Alec knew if he found the blowhole, he would also find the sheep. Alec wanted to rescue every sheep buried deep, deep in the snow.

Alec and his brothers searched through the fields, looking for a blowhole. Do you think it was hard work to find it? Alec searched and searched. For hours, he tramped through the snow-covered fields, looking and looking. It was hard, cold work. Alec and his brothers began to get tired, but they kept going. Alec knew they had to find the sheep before the animals died.

Alec searched and searched. Then, suddenly, he saw a small hole. Snow had begun to melt around a little opening.

"Come and see!" he yelled to his fathers and brothers. "I found it!"

Alec's father and brothers started digging. Had they found the flock in time? Would the sheep still be alive? Alec and his family dug and dug.

At last, they dug through the pile of snow and found the sheep underneath. All the sheep were still alive, the big sheep and the little lambs. They had kept warm together under the snow.

Alec helped lead the sheep back to a safe place in the pasture. The little lambs tried to skip and play in the deep snow. The big sheep waded through the drifts. Alec was glad to see them safe. He was glad that God made the snow melt a little hole over the sheep so he and his family could rescue them after the blizzard.

WHAT HAPPENED LATER?

When Alec grew up, he discovered a special medicine. At first, he was not sure what he wanted to do. He wanted to help people as he had helped the sheep on his farm. "Should I become a doctor?" he wondered. Alec began studying medicine, but then he changed his mind. He did not

Alexander Fleming working in his laboratory in 1943

become a doctor. He became a bacteriologist. A bacteriologist is someone who studies bacteria. Bacteria can be good or bad. Bad bacteria are a kind of germ that cause people to feel sick.

Alec wanted to study bacteria so he could help people. He wanted to find a way to kill diseases and sicknesses that made people sick. God blessed Alec's work, and one day he discovered a medicine we call penicillin. Penicillin is a special medicine that helps sick people get well. Penicillin has healed thousands of people from the effects of bad bacteria.

Alec discovered this new medicine, but he did not create it. God was the one who made penicillin. Alec said, "God has given us this medicine." He knew it was a very good gift from God.

Every good gift and every perfect gift is from above, and comes down from the Father of lights.... (James 1:17)

DISCUSSION QUESTIONS

1. What country did Alec live in?
2. What happened to the sheep in the blizzard?
3. How did Alec and his family find the sheep?
4. What did Alec do when he grew up?
5. What does our Bible verse teach us?

Berlin is the capital city of Germany.

DIETRICH BONHOEFFER: ROLLER SKATES AND A VERY SAD WAR

28

A long time ago, around 1906, a boy was born in Germany. His name was Dietrich Bonhoeffer. Dietrich had three brothers and four sisters. Dietrich was one of the youngest in his family, and the littlest boy. He had a twin sister who was exactly the same age as him. Her name was Sabine (*pronounced Sabina*). Dietrich and Sabine loved to play together. They loved to help with the chores too. They wanted to be just like their older brothers and sisters and do everything they did. Do you remember what twins are? Twins are two little babies born at exactly the same time.

Dietrich's father and mother were glad their children wanted to help. Dietrich loved to do a good job with his chores. His father wrote a note about him when he was six. He wrote, "Dietrich always wants to be useful, and he learns things very quickly."

Dietrich's father was a doctor. In 1912, he moved his family to a big city called Berlin. Berlin is the capital of Germany. Mr. Bonhoeffer had a new job in Berlin. He bought a big house for his family to live in near his new job. The house was near a zoo. Do you think the Bonhoeffer children liked to walk to the zoo to see the animals?

Dietrich was six years old when his family moved to Berlin. He was so excited to see their new house. Dietrich was even more excited when he looked out the front door. What do you think he saw? A big smooth paved area! It was perfect for roller skating. Dietrich smiled a big smile. He wanted to roller

A jaguar from South America plays with a zookeeper at the Berlin Zoo.

skate. Do you know how to roller skate? Dietrich did not know how, but his older brothers knew, and they could teach him. His brothers were named Karl-Friederich, Walter, and Klaus. They were much older than he was. Dietrich's brothers helped him, and he practiced and practiced on the street in Berlin. Soon he could roller skate all by himself.

A SAD TIME

When Dietrich was eight years old, a sad thing happened. Someone killed a man in a country called Austria. (Austria is near Germany; do you see it on the map? It is the little orange country.) The Austrians got angry. People in Russia got angry too. Then the ruler in Germany got angry. Soon people in one country began to fight people in another country. Before long, many countries were fighting each other. France and Britain started fighting Austria and Germany. A big war started. We call it World War I.

This was a sad time in Germany. Dietrich's older brothers, Karl-Friederich, Walter, and Klaus were drafted. Do you know what that means? It meant they had to

Dietrich Bonhoeffer: Roller Skates and a Very Sad War

leave their family and their home. They had to leave for the war and fight for Germany. Dietrich was too little to fight. He stayed home, far away from the fighting. He stayed with his mother, father, and sisters.

Many people got hurt in the war. Many people died. Do you think Dietrich was afraid? Do you think he worried about his brothers and wondered if they would get hurt?

For four years, people kept fighting. Then one day, Mr. Bonhoeffer received a letter. The letter had terrible news. Dietrich's brother, Walter, had died in the fighting. Dietrich's mother began to cry when she heard the news. Then the family began to cry. This was a sad time for Dietrich's family.

HOPING IN GOD

Dietrich was very sad to lose his brother Walter. One day, after the war was over, Dietrich read Psalm 42 and wrote a song about it. Dietrich's song helped him remem-

Modern re-enactment of soldiers in World War I

ber that he should trust God. He should trust God even when bad things happen. Psalm 42 says:

> Why are you cast down, O my soul,
> and why are you in turmoil within me?
> Hope in God; for I shall again praise him,
> my salvation and my God.
> (Psalm 42:5-6 ESV)

Dietrich did not understand why his brother Walter died in the war. But he knew that God was very wise and very smart. God knew what to do, so Dietrich trusted Him. He trusted Him even when sad things happened.

WHAT HAPPENED LATER?

When Dietrich grew up, he became a pastor and a teacher in Germany. He also wrote many books.

Dietrich Bonhoeffer (in dark jacket) with students

One day you may read something he wrote. No matter what happened, Dietrich Bonhoeffer knew that God was in control. He knew God would take care of him, and he trusted in God.

Why are you cast down, O my soul,
and why are you in turmoil within me?
Hope in God; for I shall again praise him,
my salvation and my God.
(Psalm 42:5-6 ESV)

DISCUSSION QUESTIONS

1. What did Dietrich learn to do when his family moved to Berlin?
2. Do you remember the name of the war that Dietrich's brothers fought in?
3. What did Dietrich do when he was sad?
4. What does our Bible verse teach us?

Mountains of Romania

SABINA WURMBRAND SUFFERS FOR JESUS

29

This is the story of a woman who loved Jesus. This woman loved Jesus so much that she suffered many things for Him. Her name was Sabina, and she lived in a country called Romania. Before we read about Sabina, we will learn more about her country.

Look at the map on this page. Can you find Romania? It is on the eastern side of Europe.

For many years, followers of Christ were free in Romania. They could meet together for church. They could sing together in worship. They could talk together with ease. But one year, all of that changed. In 1944, something terrible happened. That year, the communists took over Romania.

Who were the communists?

The communists were a group of men who took over many countries. They wanted to control the governments of Russia and other countries. They said, "This will be our country now! We will make the rules!" First, the communists took Russia's government. They took control of Russia in 1917.

In 1917, people all over Russia began to fight each other. When different people in one nation start fighting each other, we call it a civil war. The communists won the war in Russia. They took over Russia and made it their own.

The communists did not believe in God. They were atheists. They wanted all the Russian

Vladimir Lenin, leader of the communists in Russia

people to stop believing in God. They began arresting pastors and killing them. They tried to stop people from worshiping the Lord. In the schools, they told the children, "God does not exist. Only the communists can take care of you."

Do you know why some people want to believe God is not real? Some people say God does not exist because they want to be free to do whatever they want. If there is no God, they think that no one can stop them from doing what they want.

About twenty years later, another war began. This time, the war was all over the world. This war was called World War II. The communists in Russia fought the Nazis in Germany. Many other nations in Europe became a part of the war too. They became battlegrounds for the communists and the Nazis. Romania was one of those countries.

In 1944, the communists took control of Romania. They marched into the country, and one by one, they invaded its cities. Then, they celebrated their victory. They gathered church leaders from all over Romania. Pastors and priests came, from one end of the country to the other. Then, the communists held a special meeting. Joseph Stalin, their leader, was at the meeting. The church leaders praised Stalin. They praised the communists for their victory.

But remember, the communists did not believe in God. They taught that people should only put their trust in the government. So why did the pastors and priests celebrate and praise communism? Many of these church leaders had rejected King Jesus. They had become lost and forgotten what they believed. They knew the communists did not like Christians. Some of the pastors were afraid of being hurt. "Will we go to prison if we say we love God?" they thought. This is why many of the pastors were not loyal to King Jesus.

Joseph Stalin, leader of the communists in 1944

But there was a pastor at the meeting who knew that this was wrong. He remembered that we should praise Jesus and not the communists. His name was Richard Wurmbrand, and his wife's name was Sabina. Do you know what Sabina told her husband at the meeting? "Richard," she said, "Stand up and wash away this shame from the face of Christ! They are spitting in His face."

"But Sabina," Richard said, "if I do that, you will lose your husband. I will probably go to jail."

Sabina answered, "I don't want to have a husband who is a coward."

Richard knew that Sabina was right. He needed to stand up for Jesus. He needed to tell everyone that Jesus Christ was King of kings and Lord of lords. He needed to help the communists see that they were wrong. So Richard got up and went to the front of the room. Then, he began to speak.

Richard praised God. He said, "We must be loyal to God first. Jesus Christ is King." Do you think he was scared? He may have been scared, but he chose to be bold. The communists were not happy. They shut off his microphone before he could say any more. But it was too late. The radio had been on! Richard's words echoed through every house in Romania, and the communists could not stop him. All over, people heard the truth. They heard Richard's voice saying, "We must praise God, not man!" and they listened.

Do you think Richard got in trouble for this?

Yes, he did get in trouble. But he was not arrested by the communists right away.

One day, four years later, the communist police came and found Richard. In 1948, they took Richard from his home and arrested him. They took him to prison while Sabina was gone. Sabina and her son returned home, but they could not find Richard. They looked and looked and looked, but he was gone. They looked for him at the police station. "Have you seen my husband?" Sabina asked. But the police lied. "No," they said. "We have no record of him."

People all over Romania heard Pastor Wurmbrand on the radio.

What could Sabina do? She became very sad. She did not know whether her husband was alive or dead. And now, she and her son were alone. But God had made Sabina strong. She loved God, and she knew that sometimes we have to suffer for Him. She prayed for God's help.

Richard was in prison for the next fourteen years. Living in prison was hard. Richard was hurt in prison. He was hungry all the time. He was beaten many times by the communists. The prison guards were very cruel to Richard. "Deny God or we will hurt you," they said. "How could I deny my Lord?" Richard asked. He preached about Jesus night and day in prison. He praised Jesus even when he was hurt by the guards.

The Lord gave spiritual strength to Richard and the other Christians in jail. In fact, the Holy Spirit gave the Christians so much strength and power that something wonderful happened. They began to love their enemies! They prayed for their enemies. This is what Jesus commanded those who love Him to do (Matthew 5:44-45).

What do you think Sabina did while her husband was in prison?

She met with the Christians in secret. She read the Bible with them. They prayed and prayed together. "One day," they said, "we will be free again! Until then, we will be faithful to our King."

One day, about two years later, the police broke into Sabina's home again. This time, they arrested her. They asked her many questions. Then, they told her, "We will free you and your husband. But first, give us the information we need." The police commanded Sabina to tell on her friends. "Where are the other Christians?" they asked. "We need to know."

Sabina refused. She would suffer for Jesus rather than betray her fellow Christians.

The communists put Sabina into a prison camp. She worked long, long days in prison. She worked in the sun, and she worked in the cold. She dug holes and moved dirt in wheelbarrows. She was hungry all the time, and she grew very thin. The prison guards hurt Sabina just like they hurt her husband.

But God had a purpose in Sabina being there. Joseph, in the Bible, was thrown into prison. But God had a purpose in that too.

Sabina talked with as many prisoners as she could. She told them about the Lord Jesus. Many of the people in prison did not believe in God. They had no hope and nothing to give them strength. God used Sabina's testimony to give prisoners hope and joy.

Before Sabina went to prison, she memorized many Bible verses. Do you like to memorize the Bible? One day, you may need every one of those verses. Sabina did not have a printed Bible, but she could tell others what it said. This is because she had so much of it in her

Richard spent 14 years in prison.

head. Soon, many prisoners knew large parts of the Bible. They could recite the verses Sabina had learned. God used Sabina to save people in this dark place.

At last, Sabina was released from prison. But the communists warned her, "If you start religious activities again, you will be arrested."

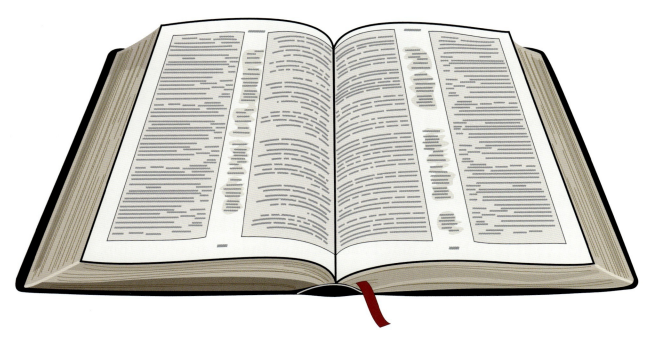

Sabina ignored the warning. "I will serve my King Jesus no matter what they say!" she thought. And because she served Jesus, Sabina could not be silent. She could not deny the Savior she loved with all her heart. She began meeting with Christians again. She began to share the Bible with others and memorize more verses.

After many years, the prison guards released Richard too. God brought him back to his wife and son. Richard and Sabina continued their mission activities. They kept meeting with other Christians and telling others about Jesus.

The communists threatened the Wurmbrands again and again. "We will take you back to prison!" they warned. But they never did. The Lord had other plans. He protected Richard and Sabina. And something wonderful happened in the 1960s. Christians all over the world paid a ransom to the communists. They paid the ransom so that the Wurmbrands could leave Romania.

Richard and Sabina did not leave Romania because they were afraid. They left because other Christians wanted to hear their stories. "You must tell the stories of suffering Christians all over the world," these people told them. "You must be the voice of the persecuted church." So that is what Richard and Sabina did.

Have you heard of The Voice of the Martyrs? Richard and Sabina created this ministry. They wanted Christians all over the world to pray for the persecuted, and to provide for their needs. They did this important work for many years. They gladly gave their whole lives in service for their King. In 2000, Sabina died and went to be with the Lord. She had lived a full life. The next year, Rich-

Richard and Sabina Wurmbrand

ard finished his work on earth too. He also went to be with Jesus and live with Him forever.

The Bible says we should remember Christians who suffer for Jesus. We should pray for them and help them however we can.

Remember the prisoners as if chained with them—those who are mistreated—since you yourselves are in the body also. (Hebrews 13:3)

DISCUSSION QUESTIONS

1. In what country did Sabina live?
2. How did Sabina give other prisoners hope?
3. What ministry did Richard and Sabina create?
4. What does our Bible verse teach us?

Brasov, Romania

The Panama Canal

A FIGHT WITH MOSQUITOES: WILLIAM GORGAS IN PANAMA

Have you sailed on a ship in the ocean? Long ago, people sailed on ships between countries. Big ships and little ships carried people to places far, far away. Today, if you want to travel to Europe, a plane can take you there! In the past, ships were the only option. Ships traveling between England and California took a long time to get there. The ships from England had to sail all the way past the tip of South America, then all the way back up to California.

People wanted to travel faster from one place to another. They decided to build a big ditch across Panama. Do you see Panama on the map? It has a blue star on it. If

A ship sailing through the Panama Canal

Panama had a big ditch crossing it, what do you think would happen? The problem would be solved! Ships could sail through the ditch. Ships could sail from the Atlantic Ocean to the Pacific Ocean without sailing around South America. The men who built the trench called their project the Panama Canal. A canal is a big ditch filled with water.

How many people do you think it would take to dig a ditch all the way across Panama from one ocean to the other? At first, the French people thought they could dig the ditch. They sent thousands and thousands of men to Panama to start digging. But soon the men got sick. Many of the men died. Then, the French stopped digging the canal.

After the French stopped, the Americans decided to start digging the canal. But they did not want to get sick. They did not want to die like the French people had. They brought a doctor with them. His name was William Crawford Gorgas, but his friends called him Willie. Willie was from Alabama in the United States.

People from the United States came to dig a canal all the way across Panama, from Colon to Panama City.

When Willie came to Panama, he took a walk to see what the country was like. All around him were tall trees and thick jungles. Beautiful birds lived in the trees, and bugs and many mosquitoes lived in the jungles too.

When Willie went to the city where he would be staying, he saw more mosquitoes flying around. The little insects lived everywhere. They lived in people's kitchens. They lived in people's bedrooms. They swarmed through the warm streets at night.

"This is the problem," said Willie. He pointed at the mosquitoes flying around.

"But it's just a little mosquito," his friend said.

"But this little mosquito is causing a big problem," Willie said. "People are getting sick because of bites from these little bugs. The mosquitoes have a strong poison in them that is not good for humans. They carry diseases. Mosquitoes love to bite people, but people do not love the sickness that follows."

Willie was right. The mosqui-

When Willie came to Panama, he saw beautiful birds and little mosquitoes everywhere.

toes in Panama were dangerous. They carried bad diseases. They carried yellow fever and malaria. Have you heard of these diseases? They often kill people. A mosquito bite was not just itchy here. It could be deadly.

"What are you going to do?" asked his friend.

"I'm going to get rid of all the mosquitoes," Willie replied.

When Willie's friend heard this, he laughed. "You can't kill all these mosquitoes!" he exclaimed. "There are millions of them! How could you possibly kill all these tiny little bugs? They can hide anywhere. You'll never be able to get rid of them all."

Willie smiled. "Perhaps not," he said. "But I'm going to try."

Willie knew it would not be easy to kill all the mosquitoes. There were millions swarming through the city. But he had an idea. What do you think his idea was?

First, Willie told everyone to put screens on their windows and doors. The screens stopped the mosquitoes from flying inside houses. The screens stopped them from biting people while they were eating or sleeping.

Then, Willie said, "Mosquitoes need water to stay alive. If we take away the water, we will take away the homes for the

Dr. Willie Gorgas was a friend to all the people who lived in Panama. Every night, he would kneel down and ask God to help him stop the sicknesses that the mosquitoes carried. God heard Willie's prayer, and He showed Willie how to get rid of the mosquitoes.

A Fight with Mosquitoes: William Gorgas in Panama

Mosquitoes live in water until they are old enough to fly and bite people. Willie Gorgas had to dump out all the water so the mosquitoes wouldn't live there.

mosquitoes. They will die, and no more will come to live here." Mosquitoes liked to live in little containers filled with water. They liked flower pots and pans and buckets. The more murky the water was, the more they felt at home.

Willie walked through the cities and towns of Panama. He found flowerpots that were full of rainwater. "Dump out that water!" he said. "We don't want mosquitoes living in it!"

Willie got lots of people to help him. They walked around every city and town in Panama. They searched through every street. If they found a bucket or barrel filled with water in the street, they dumped it.

Willie asked everyone to help. Even little children could help dump out water. They could keep their toys inside so they would not fill with water when it rained. If you lived in Panama, how would you help?

What do you think happened when all the water was dumped out? The mosquitoes stopped living in the cities and towns. Then, people stopped getting sick.

The men could work hard now that they were healthy. They could work hard digging ditches for the canal. Willie and his friends were excited to finish the canal. They cheered! "We must give this a try," they said. They climbed into a canoe and paddled from one side to the other. They paddled the whole length of the Panama Canal. Paddle, paddle, paddle they canoed from the Pacific Ocean to the Atlantic Ocean.

WHAT HAPPENED LATER?

When the canal was finished in 1914, everyone was happy. People in Panama and in other countries thanked the workers. They thanked these men who had worked hard to dig the canal. But they thanked Dr. Willie Gorgas too. Dr. Gorgas had done something very special. He had kept the workers safe. He had killed the mosquitoes that brought terrible diseases with them.

Willie knew the mosquitoes were

These were some of the men who helped dig the Panama Canal.

a dangerous enemy. He was glad that God gave us ways to fight the mosquito. When we take care of God's earth and help people live better, like Willie did, this is called *taking dominion*. God told Adam and Eve to take care of the earth and everything on it. That is what Willie Gorgas did in Panama. We should do the same with the things in our lives today.

Then God blessed them, and God said to them, "Be fruitful and multiply; fill the earth and subdue it; have dominion over the fish of the sea, over the birds of the air, and over every living thing that moves on the earth." (Genesis 1:28)

DISCUSSION QUESTIONS

1. Why did people want to build the Panama Canal?
2. What did Willie Gorgas see when he came to Panama?
3. How did Willie get rid of the mosquitoes?
4. What does our Bible verse teach us?

Gulf Islands National Seashore

Jim Sledge and a Special Pet

31

Jim was a little boy who lived in Florida. Florida is in the southern United States. Can you find Florida on the map?

Jim was born in 1924. His full name was James Seymour Sledge, but everybody called him Jim. Jim lived in a little town called Monticello. His daddy was a farmer. When Jim turned seven years old, something exciting happened. Jim's father was chosen to be the sheriff.

Do you know what a sheriff is? A sheriff is someone who protects us. Sheriffs arrest people who do naughty

Jim Sledge as a one-year-old

things. They keep everyone safe. Once in a while, Jim went to work with his daddy. He sat in his daddy's big chair. He looked at all the papers on his father's fancy desk. Jim's father worked hard to keep people safe. He worked hard to protect the people in Monticello. He also took care of his family. When Jim was only a little child, his daddy started teaching him the Bible.

Every Sunday morning, Jim and his family walked down the street to the church. Jim liked to walk. He liked to watch the birds playing and singing in the oak trees. He liked to smell the fresh grass and the wildflowers blowing in the wind. It was a beautiful walk to church. When they got there, Jim and his family would worship God and learn more about Him.

Oak trees in Florida Panhandle

GOING ON A TRIP

Jim had an uncle named Teddy Sledge. Uncle Teddy was an officer in the United States Army. One day, in 1940, the army ordered Uncle Teddy to travel to the Philippines. The army needed him to build special forts and buildings. (The Philippines is a group of islands in the Pacific Ocean. They are near China and Japan.) Uncle Teddy invited Jim to go with him on this long trip.

Jim was excited to go. He traveled with his uncle on a big ship. First, the ship sailed south until it reached the Panama Canal. Do you remember learning about Willie Gorgas and the Panama Canal? Jim sailed all the way through the canal where Willie Gorgas used to live. Then, the ship turned north. It sailed across the ocean to the Philippines. Can you see the ship's path on the map?

While the ship sailed across the ocean, Jim stood on deck and looked out at the

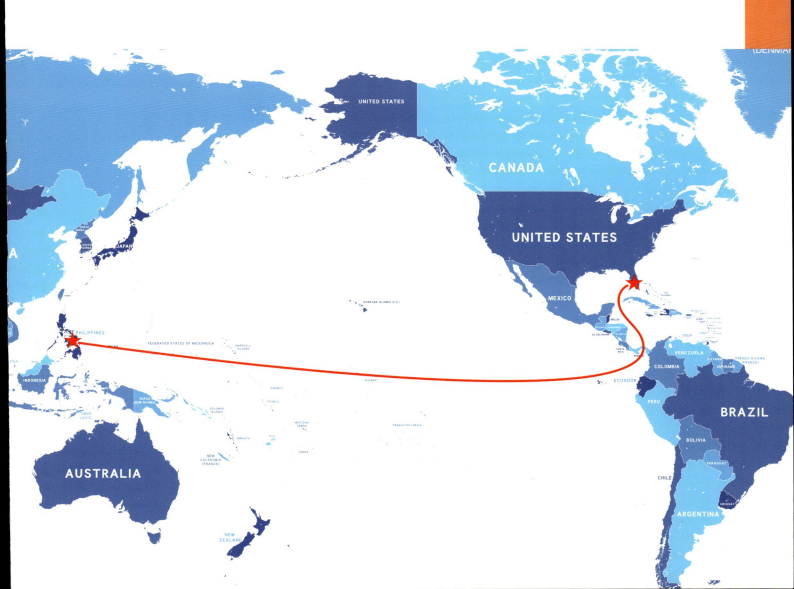

water. No matter where he looked, all he saw was water. Jim wondered why God made the ocean so big. As Jim looked, he saw fish jumping in the water. The waves sparkled as the fish swam through them. God made so many beautiful things to look at, and Jim liked looking at them.

Living in the Philippines was different than living in Florida. The Philippine islands had palm trees and white beaches to play on. Tall mountains and jungles covered the islands. Jim went to school with boys and girls from all over the world! He made friends with children from Germany, Britain, Japan, and China. Jim's new friends did not all speak English. They spoke German, Japanese, Chinese, and other languages. Jim liked to learn how to talk like his friends. Soon, Jim learned how to talk in many languages.

Jim also met the local people of the Philippines. The native children lived in the mountains. Sometimes, Jim climbed the mountains to visit his Filipino friends. Jim had never seen anything like these mountain homes. They were not like the houses Jim knew in Florida. The Filipinos did not have electricity. They used fire to cook

This Filipino family is roasting marshmallows over a fire. Has your family ever used a fire to cook food?

their food and to keep them warm. The Filipinos did not have laundry machines or dishwashers. They washed their pots and pans and clothes in the streams outside.

A NEW PET

Uncle Teddy worked in a city called Manila. Sometimes he traveled to another island called Bataan to check on the soldiers who lived there. Once, Uncle Teddy brought Jim a surprise from Bataan. What do you think it was? It was a monkey!

Jim was excited to have a monkey. Do you think you'd like a monkey for a pet? Jim did. He played with his monkey and took care of him. He named him Jerry. Each day, Jim brought the monkey food and made sure he had water to drink. Jerry loved to eat bananas. When Jim gave him a banana, Jerry would shove the whole banana in his mouth and ask for more. Jim could give Jerry several bananas, and the monkey would fit them all in his mouth at the same time.

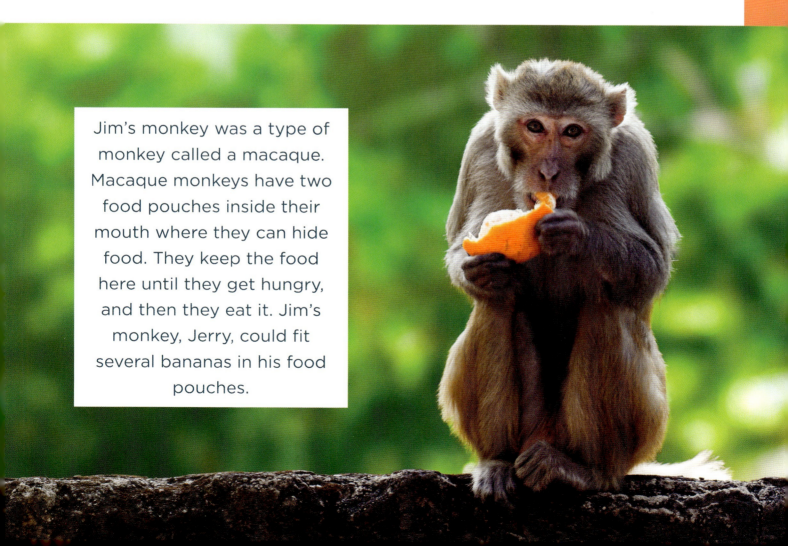

Jim's monkey was a type of monkey called a macaque. Macaque monkeys have two food pouches inside their mouth where they can hide food. They keep the food here until they get hungry, and then they eat it. Jim's monkey, Jerry, could fit several bananas in his food pouches.

When Jim grew up, he became a dentist.

"You're a silly monkey!" Jim laughed. He was amazed at all the bananas Jerry could fit in his mouth. "God gave you a very special mouth!" he told the monkey.

WHAT HAPPENED LATER?

When Jim grew up, he became a dentist. He fixed people's teeth. If a little boy or girl had trouble with one of their teeth, Jim Sledge would help them. Some children do not like to go to the dentist. Dr. Jim made dental visits fun. All the children loved Dr. Jim. He told them stories about his pet monkey, and he sang songs to them while he worked on their teeth.

The children loved to talk to Dr. Jim because he had such good stories to tell. Jim told lots of stories. He told the children about the amazing things God had made and done. "God made everything," he explained. "He made all the world and all the animals, and He cares for each one of them. And even though you can't see God, He can see you. He sees you all the time, even when you're scared or in trouble. God takes care of all the things He created, and He even takes care of you!"

Doctor Jim Sledge

For you formed my inward parts;

you knitted me together in my mother's womb.

I praise you, for I am fearfully and wonderfully made.

Wonderful are your works;

my soul knows it very well.

(Psalm 139:13-14 ESV)

DISCUSSION QUESTIONS

1. Where did Jim grow up?
2. What did Jim's daddy do?
3. What happened when Jim went to the Philippines?
4. What did Jim tell the children when he was a dentist?
5. What does our Bible verse teach us?

Hiroshima, Japan

MYEKO NAKAMURA'S HOUSE FALLS DOWN 32

How old are you? Myeko Nakamura was five years old in 1945. She lived with her family in a city in Japan called Hiroshima. She had an older brother named Toshio and an older sister named Yaeko. They lived in a little house in the city with their mother.

When Myeko was a baby, a war began between Japan and America. This war was called World War II. Myeko's father joined the Japanese soldiers in the war. He died fighting. Now, Myeko only had a mother and her brother and sister left.

Myeko's mother was a seamstress. She made clothes and sold them. When she sold the clothes, she used the money to buy food for her children. Myeko liked to watch her mother sew. Mrs. Nakamura had a sewing machine, and she used it to

Mrs. Nakamura made beautiful dresses to sell.

make beautiful clothes. She made clothes for men, and colorful dresses for ladies. The dresses were called kimonos. Myeko could hardly wait until she could help make beautiful dresses too. Do you think she liked to play with the colorful fabrics?

A SCARY DAY

One day, Myeko's brother Toshio ran into the room where she was sitting with her mother.

"The American bombers are coming!" he cried. "I hear the air raid sirens!"

Bombers were big airplanes from America. They flew over the cities in Japan and dropped bombs. The bombs destroyed buildings and killed many people. Myeko was afraid of them.

Mrs. Nakamura picked up some blankets and led her children out of the house. They hurried through the city to an open place with no buildings. "We'll be safe here," she said. "The bombers won't find us here." Then she spread out the blankets on the ground. "We'll sleep here tonight," she told the children. Myeko was excited to sleep outside under the stars. Toshio hoped they would see some bombers, but no airplanes flew over them that night.

In the morning, Mrs. Nakamura took her children back to their house and gave them some peanuts to eat for breakfast.

Suddenly, a bright light filled the sky. Then the house began to shake. "A bomb is coming!" Myeko thought.

The bomb shook the whole house. The roof crashed down on top of the children. Then the walls fell over. Myeko was almost buried under boards and pieces of the roof. "Mommy, help me!" she called.

Mrs. Nakamura ran to where

Myeko Nakamura's House Falls Down

Myeko was buried. She pulled away the broken boards and roof pieces and lifted Myeko out of the pile. "Are you alright?" she asked.

"Yes," Myeko said. "I didn't get hurt." Then she heard a sound.

"Help me, Mommy!" The sound came from under the pile of boards.

"Toshio is buried!" Myeko cried.

Mrs. Nakamura dug and dug. Finally, she found Toshio and Yaeko buried deep under the pieces of roof. She helped them climb out on top of the pile.

"Are you hurt?" she asked.

"No," the children said.

"We must leave before another bomb comes," their mother told them. Swiftly, she filled a bag with clothes and led her children away from the house. They held hands as they walked down the street of their city. It was a big city. Everywhere, houses were smashed, and tall buildings had fallen to the ground. The air was filled with dust. The dust was so thick that it made the day dark.

"Mommy, why is it dark?" Myeko asked. "It isn't night yet."

Genbaku Dome, still standing today, showing damage from the bomb

"Look! There's a fire!" said Toshio. All around them, fires had started in the fallen buildings in the city.

Mrs. Nakamura led her children away from the fires. She took them to a park in the city. "Maybe we will be safe here," she said.

Myeko was glad to stop walking. She was very, very thirsty. She curled up on the ground and wrapped her arms around her tummy. "I feel sick, Mommy," she said. Toshio and Yaeko felt sick too. The bomb that fell on their city was an especially bad bomb. It was called an atomic bomb. The bomb made Myeko and her family very sick. The sickness was called radiation poisoning.

HELPING EACH OTHER

Many people came to the park to be safe. Soon the park filled with men and women and children—sick people and hurt people. Almost everyone in Myeko's city was dead or very hurt. Those who had survived felt very sick because of the atomic bomb.

Mt. Fuji in Japan

One of the men who came to the park was Kiyoshi Tanimoto. Mr. Tanimoto was a pastor of a church in Hiroshima. He loved Jesus very much. Mr. Tanimoto had been away from the city when the bomb fell. When he looked up into the sky and saw the bomb, he ran back to the city to help. He brought a bucket of water, and he gave the thirsty people water to drink. Then he helped the people who were so hurt they could not walk. He helped them escape from the fires. All day long and all night long, Mr. Tanimoto helped people. He helped the sick people, the hurt people, and the dying people. He brought all of them to the park, where he hoped they would be safe.

In the morning, Pastor Tanimoto found some rice cakes. He brought them to the people in the park. Do you think Myeko liked to eat rice cakes for breakfast? She was glad to have strong, kind people like Mr. Tanimoto helping her and her family.

Myeko's house was ruined by the bomb, but one day she would have a new house where she could live with her family.

[Jesus said:] "A new commandment I give to you, that you love one another; as I have loved you, that you also love one another. By this all will know that you are My disciples, if you have love for one another." (John 13:34-35)

DISCUSSION QUESTIONS

1. What country did Myeko live in?
2. What happened when the bomb fell on Myeko's city?
3. What did Myeko and her family do after the bomb destroyed their house?
4. How did Pastor Tanimoto show love to the people who were sick and hurt?
5. What does our Bible verse teach us?

South Korea

33
RUSSELL BLAISDELL HELPS THE CHILDREN

Russell Blaisdell was a chaplain. Do you know what a chaplain is? A chaplain is a pastor who teaches soldiers about God. A chaplain is very good at caring for people too. Chaplains help soldiers to be strong and trust God. Chaplain Blaisdell helped American soldiers fighting in the cold snow of Korea. This war was called the Korean War.

The year 1950 was a busy one for Chaplain Blaisdell. He was busy teaching the soldiers about God. He was busy listening to the soldiers, praying for them, and talking with them. He was busy doing all the things that a pastor does. But then one day, something changed.

Chaplain Blaisdell was living in a city called Seoul in Korea. The homes and buildings in Seoul were smashed, broken, and destroyed. A lot of fighting had happened in the city. Lots of people had left the city because it was dangerous.

One morning, Blaisdell and a group of soldiers rode into the city in a truck. It was a cold morning, and Blaisdell wrapped his coat tightly around himself to keep out the wind. Then, he saw something.

"Stop the truck!" he told the driver.

Blaisdell jumped out of the truck and looked down in the snow. A little boy was sitting and shivering in the snow. The boy was cold and hungry. He had no food to eat. He had no coat to keep him warm, and he had no mommy or daddy to take care of him. He was an orphan. (An orphan is a child who doesn't have a mother or father.)

Soldiers fighting in Seoul

Chaplain Blaisdell knelt down beside the little boy. "Come here," he said softly. He wrapped the boy up in his coat and carried him back to the truck. "Don't be afraid," he told the boy. "You're safe now, and we'll find some food for you so you won't be hungry anymore."

Blaisdell climbed back into the truck, and the soldiers drove on. Soon they stopped to pick up another little child. Her name was Choi Chu-ja. Just like the little boy, Choi Chu-ja had nobody to take care of her. She was so hungry that she was crying when Chaplain Blaisdell found her. He gently picked her up and carried her back to the truck. He gave her something to eat, and she stopped crying.

All over the city of Seoul, little children were shivering in the cold. They were shivering and crying because they had no food. They had

Chaplain Lt. Col. Russell Blaisdell (right) talks with some Korean orphans he is helping.

nobody to take care of them. Chaplain Blaisdell helped all the children he could find. Soon, his truck was filled with twenty orphans. These children needed a new home and a new family to take care of them. Blaisdell gave the children food to eat and a warm bed to sleep in.

The next day, he went back into the city with his truck. He found more and more orphans who needed help. Soon, he had found almost one thousand little children. Blaisdell knew he had to find a safe place for these children—somewhere that these children would be cared for while the war was going on.

These are some of the orphans Chaplain Blaisdell took care of.

AN EXCITING TRIP

It was not safe for the children to stay in the city of Seoul. More fighting was going to happen, and the children might get hurt in the war. Blaisdell found a safe place for the children to stay. The place was called Jeju Island. The island was in the ocean beside Korea. Blaisdell knew the children would be safe there, but Jeju Island was a long way away. The children could not walk there. They would need help. Blaisdell found trucks to carry the children all the way to the beach. A boat would be waiting for them on the beach. It was a long drive. How many trucks do you think it took to carry one thousand children?

When they reached the beach, the children looked out of the trucks and saw the ocean.

"How will we get across all that water?" asked one of the little boys. "We can't swim, and I don't see any boats."

"Don't worry," Blaisdell told him. "The Korean army is sending a boat to carry us across to Jeju Island."

All day long, Blaisdell and the children waited for the boat. They waited and waited and waited, but the boat never came. It was getting very cold at the beach, and the children were hungry.

"What should I do?" Blaisdell wondered. "I have to find a way to get these children across the ocean to safety. But how can we get across without a boat?"

Blaisdell did not know what to do. He prayed and asked God to protect the children and find a safe way for them to get to Jeju Island.

Then Blaisdell had an idea. If the boat would not come, he would use an airplane! Blaisdell put all the children back into trucks and brought them to the airport. Sixteen airplanes were waiting for them. The children were excited to ride on a plane. Would you be excited to ride on a plane?

The airplane pilots and the soldiers laid down straw mats for the children to sit on. Then they lifted the children into the planes. The soldiers had brought their lunches with them to eat on the flight. When they saw how hungry the children were, they gave their lunches to the children. Then a flight nurse handed out candy. She made sure all the children

American airmen lift Korean children into a plane.

had blankets to keep them warm during the flight.

Soon, everyone was loaded onto the planes, and it was time to take off. *Vroom, vroom!* the plane engines roared. Then the planes lifted off the ground and flew up into the sky. The children were on their way to safety!

When they landed on Jeju Island, the children found a new home waiting for them. A big, big house on the island became an orphanage for them to live in. Mrs. On Soon Whang, a Korean woman, helped take care of them in their new home. The children were very happy there. They never forgot the exciting plane ride that brought them to their new island home. For the rest of their lives, they also remembered Chaplain Blaisdell. They called him "the Father of a Thousand Children."

Flight nurse Mary Spivak hands out candy to the orphans.

Defend the poor and fatherless;
Do justice to the afflicted and needy.
Deliver the poor and needy;
Free them from the hand of the wicked.
(Psalm 82:3-4)

Korean children at their new home on Jeju Island. (The island was previously called Cheju-do.)

DISCUSSION QUESTIONS

1. What country was Chaplain Blaisdell working in?
2. How many children did Chaplain Blaisdell help?
3. How did the children reach Jeju Island?
4. What does our Bible verse teach us?

Waterfall in Ecuador

Dayuma: Delivered from a Life of Fear

34

Deep in the jungles of Ecuador, there lived a people group known by the name of Waorani (we say this like "wah-RAH-nee"). In their own language, this means *we the people*.

But the other people in Ecuador called them by a different name. They called them the Aucas. This word means *savages who speared*. What a scary name! This tribe was extremely violent. They killed people who were not in their tribe. They killed their own people too. And they used spears to do the killing. The Waorani lived far away from other people. They lived near a big river in the jungle. Outsiders who came near them were often killed.

Sometime in the 1930s, a little Waorani girl was born. Her name was Dayuma.

Dayuma was a scared little girl. She was afraid of the evil spirits that lived in the woods. Sometimes, she imagined she could hear them. She was afraid that they would hurt her. Dayuma was afraid of people in her tribe too. When people became angry in the tribe, they would kill each other. The Waorani people had a lot of hate and anger inside them. No wonder Dayuma was scared. She did not like to see people get hurt.

The Waorani people needed a Savior. They needed Jesus to give them joy and hope. They needed Jesus to save them from their sins of hatred and violence. But they did not know the one true God. They had never heard about Jesus. They did not know that there was a Savior who could help them.

Deep in the jungle, the tribe waited without knowing what they waited for. They needed people who would risk their lives to save theirs. Who would be brave enough to bring the good news about God's love to the Waorani?

It was not easy to visit this violent tribe in the jungle. Nobody knew how to speak their language. How would the Waorani hear the good news? They would not understand! And the violence of the tribe made even the bravest missionaries scared. This tribe did not like visitors. In fact, they nearly always killed them.

But there were five missionaries who had strong faith. They wanted to bring the good news to the Waorani. They would go even if it cost them their lives. These five men loved God, and they loved this violent tribe. They wanted the Waorani to hear about Jesus. Their names were Jim Elliot, Nate Saint, Ed McCully, Peter Fleming, and Roger Youderian.

Nate was a pilot who had a small yellow plane. He and the other missionaries started to drop gifts over the Waorani villages. They thought, "If we bring them gifts, they will know that we will not hurt them."

Then, one day, the five missionaries decided to go together and try to meet the Waorani.

Nate Saint with his plane

Do you think the Waorani treated them with kindness? No, they did not.

The Waorani people rushed out of the jungle with their spears. They killed all five men on the banks of the river. They did not know the men wanted to help them. They did not know that Jesus could save them. The wives of these men were heartbroken when they heard what happened. "Now, our men are killed, and this tribe still needs Jesus!" they said. But two of the women who heard about the men would not give up.

One of these women was Elisabeth Elliot. She was the widow of Jim Elliot. Elisabeth lived in Ecuador with her daughter, Valerie. She had stayed at the mission house while her husband went to the jungle. The other woman was Rachel Saint. She was the sister of Nate Saint with the little yellow plane. Elisabeth and Rachel wanted to see the mission succeed. They wanted the Waorani to be saved. They wanted them to love Jesus Christ.

Now, we will go back to Dayuma's story. As a little girl, Dayuma saw a lot of hate and fear. One day, she was so scared, she decided to run away from home. She ran and ran and found a place to live with a family in Ecuador. She learned how to speak the language in Ecuador. She learned the Quichua language. For eight years, Dayuma lived with her new family and left behind her old life. She forgot about her Waorani people and the life she had once lived.

Rachel Saint

But Dayuma did not forget her fear. She grew from a scared little girl into a scared young woman. And she was angry too. She was angry because an evil man had killed her father. She wanted revenge. She wanted to hurt the man that had killed her father.

Eight years after Dayuma left her people, Rachel Saint heard about her. Rachel wanted to learn the language of the Waorani. But how could Rachel learn this difficult language?

One day, she met Dayuma. Rachel asked Dayuma to teach her the language of the Waorani.

"I have forgotten my language!" said Dayuma. "But I will try to remember!" Soon, the words came back to her. Faster and faster they filled her head. Before long, she could teach Rachel all the sounds of her language. Rachel and Dayuma met every week. Every week, Rachel got a little better. Soon, she could speak in the Waorani language too.

Jaguar in the jungles of Ecuador

"Why does this woman from America want to know my language?" wondered Dayuma. "Why have you come here?" she asked.

Rachel told Dayuma, "I came so that I can put God's carving into your language and teach your people what He says."

Rachel meant that she had come to bring the Bible to the Waorani. "I want to translate the Bible into your language," she told Dayuma. I want your people to be able to read it and hear it for themselves. Do you know why Rachel called it a *carving*? The Waorani did not have books. They carved markings on trees.

As Rachel learned the new language, she told Dayuma about Jesus. Rachel told Dayuma that God created all things. All the things God created were very beautiful! But then the people began to sin. They did bad things and a big space formed between them and God. Rachel explained that all people need a Savior. We need someone who can take care of our sin for us. She told Dayuma that we have a Savior. His name is Jesus. "God loves us!" she said, "And He wants to be close to us. He sent His son Jesus to save us and give us new life."

"Who is this man I have never heard of?" wondered Dayuma. "Who is this man that came from heaven to earth? And why did He come? What did He do when He was here on earth?"

Dayuma had been afraid of the evil spirits hiding in the dark jungle. She was afraid of those evil spirits harming her. But now, she was excited. "Here is someone who is stronger than the evil spirits!" she thought. "This man called Jesus can cast out demons!"

Dayuma listened as Rachel told her stories about Jesus. Rachel told the story of Jesus casting demons out of the man of the Gadarenes. Do you remember this story? As Dayuma listened, she became even more excited. Jesus told the man who was set free:

"Return to your own house, and tell what great things God has done for you." (Luke 8:39)

Dayuma thought, "If God frees me from fear and evil spirits, I must go back to my people. I must tell them about this God who is so powerful."

Before Dayuma went back to her tribe, she visited America with Rachel. She decided to follow Jesus when she was in America. She gave her life to His care. She was baptized too. Dayuma was the first Waorani to believe the good news about Jesus. Rachel was filled with happiness. All over America, Christians cheered when they heard about Dayuma. "The Waorani people will finally know the love of Jesus!" they said.

Then, Rachel and Dayuma went back to Ecuador. Dayuma was ready. She was ready to find her family and tell them about Jesus the Savior.

At last, after a long journey, Dayuma found her family. Her mother, Akawo, was still alive. Some of her other family members were still alive too. They were happy to see Dayuma. They cried tears of joy.

Dayuma told her people about the outsiders. She told them how kind they were. And she told them about the missionaries. She said they had come to bring them good news about Jesus. Dayuma began to explain all that she had learned about the Bible from Rachel Saint. The Waorani gathered each week to listen. They loved to hear Dayuma tell stories from the Bible. Soon, the Waorani knew the name of Jesus. They learned more and more about Jesus. They learned that He had come to save people like them.

Dayuma's baptism

Dayuma also explained God's law to her people. She told them about the Ten Commandments. Dayuma explained, "God says you should not spear people. It is a sin to spear people. And it is a sin to tell others to do it, even if you do not do it."

Can you guess what happened next? Rachel Saint and Elisabeth Elliot went to live with the Waorani. Rachel knew the language well now. In 1965, she finished translating the Gospel of Mark. The Christians in the world were excited when they heard this. Now, the Waorani could read part of the Bible in their own language! The Waorani were excited too. It was a great blessing to be able to read and understand God's Word.

Dayuma sharing God's Word

As the years passed, more and more people in the tribe trusted Jesus. They repented from their sins. Jesus took away the hate in their hearts and filled them with love. God had mercy on this special tribe. He used people like Dayuma and Rachel to bring the good news of Jesus to them. He took away the darkness from their hearts.

God was kind to the Waorani by saving them and giving them hope. God's Word says this in Titus 3:

For we ourselves were once foolish, disobedient, led astray, slaves to various passions and pleasures, passing our days in malice and envy, hated by others and hating one another. But when the goodness and loving kindness of God our Savior appeared, he saved us.... (Titus 3:3-5a ESV)

> **DISCUSSION QUESTIONS**
> 1. What is the name of Dayuma's tribe?
> 2. In what country did this tribe live?
> 3. Who learned to speak Waorani by spending time with Dayuma?
> 4. What does our Bible passage teach us?

This is the end of our last story in history. But it is just the beginning of your story. How will God use you in His kingdom? What exciting things will you do for Him? How will you use your special gifts and talents to love God and others?

God is at work in the world! He is doing His will. He is saving sinners through His Son, Jesus. God is building His kingdom in the world. It is an exciting time to live and serve Him.

Remember, God made you and me for a purpose. You have a part to play in God's history. There are many things you can do in life. But there are two things that every one of us must do. First, we must always seek to bring God glory. Second, Jesus tells us that we must seek "the kingdom and His righteousness" (Matthew 6:33).

One day, Jesus will return. Then, all who trust in Him will live with Him forever! All the sad and bad things that happen in this lifetime will be forgotten. There will only be joy and peace in the life to come. Living with God will be the biggest adventure of all. That will be the end of history and the beginning of eternity!

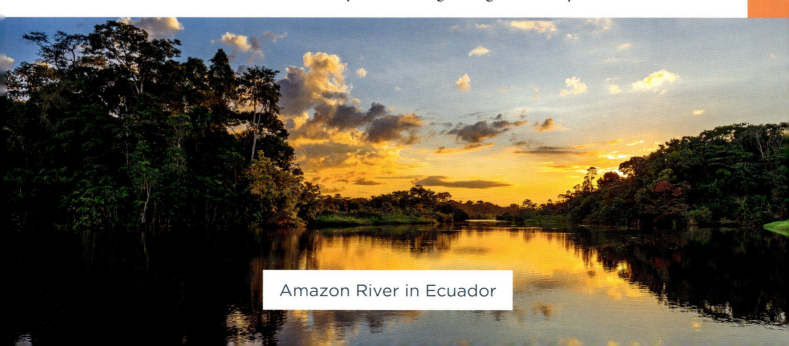

Amazon River in Ecuador

MY FIRST HISTORY

LIST OF IMAGES

Image Sources:
i – iStock.com
w – Wikimedia Commons
c – Illustration by Cedric Hohnstadt
l – Library of Congress
p – Primary Source (see Introduction)

CHAPTER 1
1. Jochebed and Miriam - c
2. Miriam - c
3. Nile River - i
4. Moses - i
5. Pyramids - i

CHAPTER 2
1. Jerusalem - i
2. Map of Mediterranean - i
3. King or Queen - i
4. Scrolls - i
5. Kids fighting - i
6. Josiah - c
7. Boy - i

CHAPTER 3
1. Donkey - i
2. Streets of Jerusalem - i
3. Peter knocking - c

CHAPTER 4
1. Patara - i
2. Map of Mediterranean - i
3. Boy and girl in ancient clothing - i
4. Girl - i
5. Statue of Constantine - i
6. Bishop Nicholas - i

CHAPTER 5
1. Camels - i
2. Pear tree - i
3. Augustine throwing pears - c
4. Pigs - i
5. Augustine - w

CHAPTER 6
1. Ural Mountains - i
2. Reindeer - i
3. Stephen of Perm - c
4. Fox and fur coats - i
5. Boy - i
6. Zyrian alphabet - w
7. Alphabet - i

CHAPTER 7
1. Nuremberg - i
2. Nightingale - i
3. Shoemaker instruments - i
4. Shoemakers - i
5. Cobbler - i
6. Hans Sachs with friends - i
7. Hans Sachs - w

CHAPTER 8
1. Lausanne - i
2. Switzerland Map - i
3. Bell - i
4. Marie pulling bell - c
5. Girl using quill pen - i
6. Marie with mother - i

CHAPTER 9
1. Nordingrå - i
2. Martin Luther - w
3. Gustav Vasa - w
4. Location of Sweden - i
5. Gustavus Adolphus - w
6. Gustavus at Breitenfeld - w

CHAPTER 10
1. Barley - i
2. English house - i
3. Horse - i
4. Isaac Newton with telescope - c
5. Isaac Newton's telescope - w
6. Apple falling - i
7. Isaac Newton - w

CHAPTER 11
1. Musical instruments - i
2. Gentlemen and ladies - i
3. Map of the world - i
4. Organ - i
5. Water Music - c
6. George Frederic Handel - w

CHAPTER 12
1. Waterfalls - i
2. Monkey and tiger - i
3. Rajanaiken - c
4. Mountains - i

CHAPTER 13
1. Persian girl 1 - i
2. Iran - i
3. Persian girl illustration - i
4. Persian desert illustration - i
5. Persian girl 2 - i
6. Fidelia Fiske - w

CHAPTER 14
1. Maui - i
2. Hawaiian Islands Map - i
3. Children on shore - c
4. Shark - i
5. Fruit - i
6. Grave marker - w

CHAPTER 15
1. Telegraph - i
2. Mailman - i
3. Studio in Charleston - w
4. James Monroe - w
5. John Adams - w
6. Marquis de Lafayette - w
7. Samuel Morse with his telegraph - c
8. Original telegraph message - l
9. Map of Maryland - i
10. Samuel Morse - w

CHAPTER 16
1. Fall in Ontario, Canada - i
2. Little girl - i
3. Little girl carrying eggs - i
4. Covered wagon - i
5. Cow herd - i
6. Susquehanna River - i
7. River crossing - i
8. Map of Canada - i

CHAPTER 17
1. Amicalola Falls State Park in Georgia - i
2. Map of United States - i
3. Elias Boudinot with printing press - c
4. Cherokee barn - i
5. Cherokee newspaper - w
6. Elias Boudinot - w

CHAPTER 18
1. Blue Ridge Mountains - i
2. McCormick Farm 1 - w
3. McCormick Farm 2 - w
4. Tractor - i
5. Farmer with scythe - i
6. Cyrus McCormick's reaper - w
7. Cyrus Hall McCormick - w
8. Tractor harvesting - i

CHAPTER 19
1. Louis Pasteur in laboratory - i
2. Mom caring for sick child - i
3. Microscope - i
4. Louis Pasteur illustration - c
5. Mouse - i
6. Joseph Meister - w
7. Louis Pasteur - w

CHAPTER 20
1. English home - i
2. Books - i
3. Church in Essex - i
4. Spurgeon preaching - c
5. Metropolitan Tabernacle - i

CHAPTER 21
1. Tokyo - i
2. Jinrikisha - i
3. Chopsticks - i
4. Cherry trees - i
5. Joseph Neesima - c

CHAPTER 22
1. Port Vila - i
2. Map of Oceania - i
3. Little girl - i
4. Vanuatu house - i
5. Church on Aniwa - w
6. Pig - i
7. Kahi and Ropu married - c
8. Vanuatu beach - i

9. Coconut - i
10. Coconut tree - i
11. Jungle forests - i

CHAPTER 23
1. Grist mill - i
2. Home of Moses Carver - w
3. Little boy with plant - i
4. Peanut diagram - i
5. George Washington Carver with Teddy - c
6. George Washington Carver - w

CHAPTER 24
1. Beach in Thailand - i
2. Map of Southeast Asia - i
3. Thai Princess - i
4. Elephant - i
5. Children - i
6. Woman in dress - i
7. Anna Leonowens - w

CHAPTER 25
1. Idanre Hills - i
2. Mary Slessor - w
3. Map of Africa - i
4. African tribesmen - i
5. African girl - i
6. Nigerian huts - i
7. Baby - i
8. Baby and cat - i
9. Mary Slessor and family - w

CHAPTER 26
1. Map of Taiwan - i
2. Japanese soldiers - w
3. Coast of Taiwan - i
4. Chi Wang - p
5. Chi Wang Memorial Church - p

CHAPTER 27
1. Ayrshire - i
2. Map of United Kingdom - i
3. Sheep - i
4. Girl with lamb - i
5. Sheep in snow - i
6. Boy with lamb - i
7. Alexander Fleming - w

8. Coast of Scotland - i

CHAPTER 28
1. Berlin - i
2. Berlin Zoo - w
3. Dietrich with brothers - c
4. World War I soldiers - i
5. Dietrich with students - w

CHAPTER 29
1. Mountains of Romania - i
2. Map of Europe - i
3. Vladimir Lenin - w
4. Joseph Stalin - w
5. Radio - i
6. Prison - i
7. Bible - i
8. Richard and Sabina Wurmbrand - w
9. Bucharest, Romania - i
10. Brasov, Romania - i

CHAPTER 30
1. The Panama Canal - i
2. Map of Route - i
3. Ship sailing through canal - i
4. Map of Panama - i
5. Toucan and mosquito - i
6. Willie Gorgas - w
7. Water in pot and wagon - i
8. Diagram - i
9. Panama Canal - w
10. Panama Canal workers - w

CHAPTER 31
1. Gulf Islands National Seashore - i
2. Map of USA - i
3. Jim Sledge (1-year-old) - p
4. Oak trees - i
5. Map of Florida to Philippines - w
6. Filipino family - i
7. Monkey - i
8. Dentist - i
9. Dr. Jim Sledge - p

CHAPTER 32
1. Hiroshima, Japan - i
2. Little girl - i

3. Japanese dresses - i
4. Map of Japan - i
5. Genbaku Dome - i
6. Mt. Fuji - i

CHAPTER 33
1. South Korea - i
2. Map of North and South Korea - i
3. Soldiers fighting - w
4. Chaplain Blaisdell with orphans - w
5. Orphans - w
6. Map of Seoul and Jeju Island - w
7. American airmen - w
8. Mary Spivak - w
9. Korean children - w
10. Cherry blossom - i

CHAPTER 34
1. Waterfall - i
2. Map of Ecuador - i
3. Nate Saint with plane - w
4. Rachel Saint - w
5. Jaguar - i
6. Dayuma's baptism - w
7. Dayuma sharing God's Word - w
8. Amazon River - i